BERDYAEV'S PHILOSOPHY:
THE EXISTENTIAL PARADOX
OF FREEDOM AND NECESSITY

Fuad Nucho

BERDYAEV'S PHILOSOPHY:
THE EXISTENTIAL PARADOX
OF FREEDOM AND NECESSITY

A CRITICAL STUDY

WITH AN INTRODUCTION BY
DR. RICHARD KRONER

LONDON
VICTOR GOLLANCZ LTD
1967

Material from *Freedom and the Spirit* by Nicolas Berdyaev. Reprinted by permission of Geoffrey Bles Ltd.

Material from *The Meaning of the Creative Act* (Victor Gollancz Ltd.), *Truth and Revelation* and *The Beginning of the End* (both Geoffrey Bles Ltd.) by Nicolas Berdyaev. Reprinted by permission of Harper & Row, Publishers.

Material from *The Destiny of Man* by Nicolas Berdyaev. Reprinted by permission of Harper & Row, Publishers and Geoffrey Bles Ltd.

Material from *Dream and Reality* by Nicolas Berdyaev. Reprinted by permission of The Macmillan Company and Geoffrey Bles Ltd.

Material from *Slavery and Freedom* by Nicolas Berdyaev, translated by R. M. French. Copyright 1944 by Charles Scribner's Sons. Reprinted by permission of Charles Scribner's Sons and Geoffrey Bles Ltd.

PRINTED IN GREAT BRITAIN BY
LOWE AND BRYDONE (PRINTERS) LIMITED, LONDON, N.W.10

Dr. Fuad Nucho's book on Berdyaev contains a highly valuable and most helpful discussion of the labyrinthine and often tortuous movements of thought we find in the many works of this Russian thinker. Berdyaev is neither a philosopher nor a theologian in the traditional sense, and yet he is both in a new sense that is quite his own.

Berdyaev was a Russian but was exiled by the Bolsheviks and lived for many years in Paris where he became a "good European" (to use Nietzsche's designation). He strove, moreover, toward universality and therefore deserves strong acclaim in an age that dwarfs all merely nationalistic thought. However, in spite of this broad horizon, Berdyaev was not an abstract "scientific" philosopher, but, as he called himself, an "existential" thinker. It is characteristic that his best book is probably his spiritual autobiography entitled *Dream and Reality*.

Dr. Nucho provides an excellent guide through the manifold aspects and subjects of Berdyaev's "theo-philosophy" by demonstrating that the idea of freedom is dominant in all its manifestations. Very skillfully he illuminates the great variety of meanings that this term embraces, and he succeeds in showing convincingly that the complicated development of Berdyaev's philosophy offers a clue to the reconciliation of the differences and appar-

ent contradictions that his concept of freedom underwent
during his life. A kind of dialectic took place in Berdyaev's
thought so that the connotation of this guiding principle
seems to be blurred. Dr. Nucho makes it clear that the
dialectical windings of Berdyaev's inner development can
fully explain this impression. In this way he is able to
systematize, as far as this is possible, the quite unsystematic fabric of thought woven by the eminent Russian.

DR. RICHARD KRONER

CONTENTS

Perhaps never before in the history of mankind has the threat to man's freedom been as great as it is in our generation. Two world wars were fought in the name of freedom. Both East and West claim to be its defenders. Freedom, however, is an elusive phenomenon, a theme with many variations, and there is no general agreement as to what constitutes it. Conflicting definitions have often divided men in their search and struggle for freedom. One of the most urgent needs in our times appears to be the clarification of the idea of freedom.

The life and thinking of Nicolas Berdyaev, the Russian religious philosopher, were steeped in the problem of freedom. This existentialist thinker spent his life "hammering out a philosophy of freedom." It was the dominant theme of his numerous writings. Berdyaev's entire life was a struggle for freedom, a struggle that led to his permanent exile from his homeland in 1922. As he tells us in his autobiography, he left Russia with the hope of finding freedom in the West; and in the West, he did indeed find freedom, freedom to live and think, to write and develop his philosophy of freedom.

But although Berdyaev wrote extensively about freedom, he did so in a rather unsystematic and seemingly ambiguous way. He never developed his philosophy into a systematic whole. The works on Berdyaev that have been published have their definite merit. However, by and large, they have treated the various aspects of his philosophy in a descriptive rather than analytic and unifying manner. Berdyaev's philosophy still needs systematization, and his concept of freedom, in particular, calls for clarification. Especially his perplexing doctrine of "uncreated freedom," the source of much misunderstanding and the target of repeated criticism, requires delineation.

The purpose of the present study is to elucidate and systematize Berdyaev's philosophy, which revolves around the existential paradox of freedom and necessity, and which he himself regarded as a philosophy of freedom. It is hoped that this work will arouse interest in further study in the manifold aspects of Berdyaev's thought, and that it will also contribute in some small measure to man's unceasing effort to understand and acquire freedom. Berdyaev's kinship to both Eastern and Western thinking may well serve to make him a bridge of understanding in our ideologically torn world. His interpretation and defense of Christianity have a striking affinity to the early Christian apologists and philosophers. Cambridge University, on the occasion of conferring upon him the honorary degree of Doctor of Divinity, referred to him as the second Socrates. The ability of this existentialist thinker to free historical Christianity of much of its anthropomorphic and sociomorphic cargo should make his philosophy particularly relevant to our scientific age.

I wish to acknowledge with deep gratitude my debt to Dr. Richard Kroner whose interest, stimulation, and encouragement made the present work possible. It has been a rare privilege to have known this great man and outstanding scholar whose life and work exemplify the victory of freedom over necessity. It is also a pleasure to express my special thanks to Mrs. Kay Scheuer, Anchor Books Editor, for her invaluable suggestions and generous help. To my wife, Aina, I am particularly grateful for her constructive comments and support given without limit in countless ways.

FUAD NUCHO

BERDYAEV'S PHILOSOPHY:
THE EXISTENTIAL PARADOX
OF FREEDOM AND NECESSITY

CHAPTER I

THE PROBLEM OF FREEDOM

1 FREEDOM AND EXISTENTIALISM

Existentialism is a revolt against traditional philosophy. Its theme is heard in several widely different variations. Forerunners of the movement can be discerned here and there in the past, but it is only recently that existentialism has gained momentum and has begun to exercise an impact upon men's life and thinking.

In its early stage, existentialism was a reaction to the Hegelian metaphysical system. Rationalism, which culminated in Hegel, had divorced reason from life. Existentialism is a protest against this artificial division. It is a denial of the assumption that logical systems are the sure way to truth. It is an assertion that the making of decisions, and not the formulation of systems, is the key to ultimate reality. The great questions of life, the existentialists insist, cannot be answered by means of scientific thinking. Man solves philosophical questions not by his thinking but by his living.

The existentialists may differ in the particular brand of their philosophies; they may disagree among themselves on the approaches to the problem they seek to solve; but they all have one objective in common, namely, the liberation of man from whatever enslaves him. They all attempt to neutralize the intellectual and social forces which are destroying man's freedom. The affirmation of the reality of human freedom and responsibility is the central theme of existentialism. The existentialist thinkers attempt, in various ways, to awaken modern man to the realities of his predicament and to arouse him to the exercise of his existential freedom. They are especially aware of the enslaving and dehumanizing influences of technology. They abhor the progressive mechanization of life. They point to the danger inherent in a technological civilization and raise the difficult question as to how modern man, without destroying the useful machine he has invented, can free himself from the alienating influences of that machine. The existentialists urge that mass uniformity must be resisted in every walk of life. They call upon the individual to think for himself and to understand himself as a free person. They advise modern man to guard and defend freedom as his birthright and to guide every action he undertakes with the light of freedom.

Existentialism is not interested in man in general, but in man the individual. Any knowledge of man must begin with his existence. It must turn to the concrete element of his life. Man expresses himself by the way he exists, by the manner he lives his life. The stress is placed on the active, concrete aspect of human existence. Man is understood through his capacity to make decisions, that is, through the use of his freedom. As a moral agent, man is free to choose what he wants to be. He is free to make himself a human being.

Practically all existentialists claim to be advocates of human freedom, but they are divided as to what constitutes the freedom they advocate. The various shades of meanings which the existentialist thinkers find in freedom may be classified under two main tendencies, the one leading to the viewpoint that freedom is incompatible with belief in God, and the other culminating in the conviction that God is the Ground of all freedom. In the first group, that of atheistic existentialism, are such thinkers as Nietzsche, Heidegger, Sartre, and Camus. The proponents of the second tendency, that of religious existentialism, are such men as Kierkegaard, Buber, Marcel, and Berdyaev.

2 FREEDOM AND BERDYAEV

Among the religious existentialists, the most outspoken champion of freedom is the Russian Orthodox philosopher Nicolas Berdyaev. It is he who has been called the "philosopher of freedom" and described as the "captive of freedom." A few quotations from Berdyaev's autobiography seem to justify these titles: "From my early childhood I was wedded to freedom."[1] "The problem which preoccupied me above every other was that of freedom."[2] "Freedom, unconditional and uncompromising, has been the fountainhead and prime mover of all my thinking."[3]

Berdyaev wrote intensively and extensively about freedom, and he wrote as an existentialist, for he regarded his philosophy to be as such. "I was an existentialist even before I came to know Kierkegaard's writings."[4] In all his writings, Berdyaev is persistently and fervently preoccupied with defending man's freedom. He is intoxicated with freedom and is constantly absorbed with the task of fighting slavery in all its forms. Yet, the concept of freedom he advocates seems invariably to be surrounded by a baffling ambiguity. The reader is struck by the abundance of vagueness in Berdyaev's references to freedom. Precise definitions are nowhere to be found. Indeed, scattered on the pages of his writings are numerous definitions of a general nature which provide little clarity. These take the form of overconcentrated equations of theological and philosophical terms, which tend to leave the reader sus-

[1] Nicolas Berdyaev, *Dream and Reality*, trans. by Katherine Lampert (New York: The Macmillan Co., 1951), p. 46
[2] *Ibid.*, p. 24
[3] *Ibid.*, p. 158
[4] *Ibid.*, p. 102

pended in the air or stranded at a dead end. Here are a
few examples: "God is freedom."[5] "Life in God is freedom."[6] "Spirit is freedom and freedom is spirit."[7] "Freedom is my own norm and my own creation of good and
evil."[8] "Freedom appeared to me as the initial, primary
reality, as the *A Priori* of existence."[9]

Berdyaev's statements on what he does not mean by
freedom are much clearer. It may be helpful to keep in
mind from the outset that, in his view, freedom is not
identical with "free will," that is, the possibility and ability to choose between alternatives. The freedom of choice
between good and evil, for instance, is not true freedom,
according to Berdyaev, because it presupposes a norm outside the person by which the distinction between good and
evil is determined. This is equivalent to external determination and, therefore, the so-called "freedom of choice"
is not real freedom.

> Freedom of will, confronted for ever with the terrifying ne-
> cessity of choosing between alternatives externally imposed
> upon it from above, represses and enslaves man . . . man is
> free when he need not choose.[10]

> For me freedom has always meant something quite different
> (from "free-will") . . . its reality does not depend on any
> norm and its exercise is not a mere choice between a good and
> an evil standing over against me . . . Liberation comes when
> the choice is made.[11]

[5] Berdyaev, *Slavery and Freedom*, trans. by R. M. French
(New York: Charles Scribner's Sons, 1944), p. 82

[6] Berdyaev, *Dream and Reality*, p. 53

[7] *Ibid.*, p. 56

[8] *Ibid.*, p. 52

[9] *Ibid.*, p. 48

[10] Berdyaev, *The Destiny of Man* (Paris, 1931), trans. by
Natalie Duddington (New York: Charles Scribner's Sons, 1937),
p. 80

[11] Berdyaev, *Dream and Reality*, p. 52

Moreover, according to Berdyaev, freedom should not be equated with, or made to depend on, individualism. Man turns to individualism in order to escape the slavery of society, but the type of individualism he often adopts turns out to be nothing but a form of slavery to his egocentric self. "Individualism demeans man."[12] "Individualism is the tragedy of empty freedom."[13] "Individualism in social life . . . establishes wolfish relations among men."[14] The individualism prevalent in capitalistic society with its stress on economic freedom and unlimited right to own private property destroys the human personality and, with it, freedom.[15] Berdyaev repeatedly insists that, contrary to popular belief, freedom is not right, but obligation. Liberals, he says, tend to regard freedom as right, not responsibility; they think of it in terms of ease, and the absence of pressure, a view that makes freedom the privilege of the ruling classes.[16] Berdyaev is equally vehement in his criticism of collectivism, especially its communist brand, which cannot but be authoritarian and "cannot admit freedom"[17] even though it strives to free man from heavy work and long hours and from "compulsory organization of labour."[18]

Berdyaev lived and fought for freedom. In a steady stream of published works he expounded an existential philosophy of freedom. "All my life," he claims in his

[12] Berdyaev, *The Meaning of the Creative Act* (Moscow, 1916), trans. by Donald A. Lowrie (New York: Harper & Brothers, 1954), p. 153

[13] *Ibid.*

[14] Berdyaev, *Slavery and Freedom*, p. 136

[15] Berdyaev, *The Destiny of Man*, p. 213

[16] Berdyaev, *The Realm of Spirit and the Realm of Caesar*, trans. by Donald A. Lowrie (New York: Harper & Brothers, 1952), p. 106

[17] *Ibid.*, p. 120 ff; cf. Berdyaev, *The Destiny of Man*, p. 212 f

[18] Berdyaev, *The Destiny of Man*, p. 213

2

autobiography, "I was engaged in hammering out a philosophy of freedom."[19] But tracing the development of his philosophy of freedom through a chronological reading of his books would yield a zigzag discourse that can be confusing. Berdyaev seems to be allergic to any systematization and repeatedly counsels his readers that freedom defies classified rationalization and eludes exact definition. Nevertheless, even unsystematic presentations, so characteristic of Berdyaev's writings, must be studied in a systematic way. Several authors have dealt with his concept of freedom but chiefly as one aspect of his thinking within the context of general surveys of his life and thought. Such studies, as it will be shown later, are descriptive rather than analytical accounts of what Berdyaev meant by freedom. The fact must be stressed that his concept of freedom cannot be studied as an isolated aspect of his thought inasmuch as it constitutes the backbone of his philosophical posture. Berdyaev propounded in an unsystematic fashion a philosophy of freedom. It is the objective of the present study to work out that philosophy into a systematic whole.

It is hoped that the methodological procedure to be adopted will enable us to place the scattered and often paradoxical pieces of Berdyaev's philosophical puzzle in their proper places and thus acquire a total and systematic picture of his thinking. It might be helpful at this point to state briefly what Berdyaev actually meant by "philosophy" in general and by "philosophy of freedom" in particular. "I am one of the most untraditional philosophers," he writes in his autobiography.[20] In his view, philosophy is an art that seeks to know the truth about man, his life and his freedom by means of intuition rather than discursive reasoning. His philosophy is not interested in the

[19] Berdyaev, *Dream and Reality*, p. 46
[20] *Ibid.*, p. 49

scientific treatment of ontological questions regarding the universe. It is preoccupied with man as an end in himself. "I have put Freedom, rather than Being, at the basis of my philosophy."[21] He regarded his philosophy as "existentialist" and, in his opinion, "true existentialist philosophy is represented by St. Augustine, Pascal, Kierkegaard and Nietzsche rather than by Heidegger, Jaspers or Sartre."[22] Berdyaev cautions us not to confuse his philosophy with what is commonly known as the "philosophy of life," with which it has nothing in common, because "there is in it no cult of life as the highest criterion."[23] Thus when he calls his existential philosophy a "philosophy of freedom," he is not using the term "philosophy" in the popular sense, meaning his general outlook about, or basic belief in, freedom; nor does he use it as equivalent to "rationale for" as the word "philosophy" usually signifies in such phrases as "philosophy of socialism," "philosophy of communism," or "philosophy of democracy." Philosophy, as Berdyaev conceived of it, occupies a place between religion and science and, therefore, in its methods and objectives it should not try to imitate either one. It will become clearer in the course of this study that Berdyaev's conception of philosophy is uniquely his own. Perhaps it will suffice to conclude this preliminary section with one of his best definitions of philosophy: "Philosophy is the art of knowing in freedom by creating ideas which resist the given world and necessity and penetrate into the ultimate essence of the world."[24]

[21] Berdyaev, *Dream and Reality*, p. 46
[22] *Ibid.*, p. 93
[23] Berdyaev, *The Beginning and the End* (Paris: 1947), trans. by R. M. French (London: Geoffrey Bles, 1952), p. 48
[24] Berdyaev, *The Meaning of the Creative Act*, p. 29

3 METHODOLOGY

The study must naturally begin with an analysis of the "formative influences" which molded the existential thinking of Berdyaev. The most significant highlights in his life will be illuminated. The determining factors of Russian history and destiny will be discussed. The impact of Russian Orthodoxy on his thinking will then be investigated. This will be followed by an assessment of the molding influence exercised by the Russian literary currents, especially that of Tolstoy and Dostoyevsky. This chapter will conclude with an attempt to trace Berdyaev's philosophical roots. His alleged philosophical kinship to Vladimir Solovyev, Jacob Boehme, Immanuel Kant, and Sören Kierkegaard will be considered.

The following chapter will deal with Berdyaev's fundamental paradox, freedom and necessity, which underlies all his philosophical thought. The first step here will be to outline Berdyaev's philosophical anthropology. If his preoccupation with freedom arises, as he says, out of his interest in man, it follows that his presuppositions about man must first be brought to light. The conflict between freedom and necessity will also be analyzed and described as it is waged in nature, society, civilization and history.

The fourth chapter will be devoted to the implications of the basic paradox of freedom and necessity. This will call for a study of Berdyaev's conception of personality and its vital relationship to freedom. The principle of objectification will be investigated, and the phenomena of depersonalization and dehumanization will be discussed. The chapter will be concluded by an analysis of individualism and collectivism and their effects on the human personality.

The subsequent chapter will focus upon the concept of creativity, which is a cornerstone in the philosophical structure of Berdyaev. The nature of creativeness will be reviewed, and the role of creativity in ethics, art and philosophy will be examined.

In the sixth chapter, entitled "Freedom and Spirituality," the vital topics of symbolism, mysticism, revelation, metahistory and eschatology will be considered, and the possibility of the solution of the paradox of freedom and necessity will be investigated.

The purpose of the seventh chapter will be to attempt a statement of Berdyaev's philosophy as a philosophy of freedom. This will require an analysis of the meaning or meanings of his concept of freedom in the light of the entire study, with due sensitiveness to the dynamic development of his thought.

The final chapter will be devoted to criticisms and evaluations of Berdyaev's philosophy of freedom.

CHAPTER II

FORMATIVE INFLUENCES

1 BIOGRAPHICAL HIGHLIGHTS

Nicolas Alexandrovitch Berdyaev was born in Kiev in 1874. His father came of a long line of military men, chiefly generals, and was himself an officer in the Imperial Guards. His mother, born Princess Kudashev, was half-French and also related to the Polish nobility. By birth, she was Orthodox but "felt herself to be more of a Roman Catholic."[1] Thus from the very beginning Berdyaev enjoyed the advantages of a broad cultural heritage. Reared in a predominantly French household in a Russian milieu, his sensitive soul and brilliant mind were exposed to a colorful and in some ways clashing assortment of influences.

Continuous illness at home, especially of his mother, was a source of much distress for the young Berdyaev. He himself developed quite early in his life what is known as *tic douloureux*, a nervous condition of the facial muscles accompanied by severe neuralgic pains. This chronic ailment caused him a great deal of discomfort and embarrassment throughout his life.

Berdyaev's early education at the Military Cadet Corps of Pages, an exclusive academy, instilled in him a dislike for all regimentation. The six years he spent in this school intensified his longing for freedom from rules and regula-

[1] Berdyaev, *Dream and Reality*, p. 3

tions and helped develop in him resistance to conformity
to any collective. He did not particularly like the "worldly
society of the upper class" and he "longed for a complete
break."[2]

In 1894, when he was a law student at Kiev University,
Berdyaev's concern for social justice made him turn to
Marxism. His participation in political agitation led to his
deportation to Vologda. His expulsion from the university meant the end of his formal education, and while he
later pursued his studies independently, he never earned
a degree. When he began writing, he was still struggling to
free himself from materialistic Marxism, although Ibsen
and Dostoyevsky, whose writings he read in the meantime,
helped him recognize Marxism's philosophical weaknesses.
He wrote his first book, *Subjectivism and Individualism in
Social Philosophy*, during his political exile in Vologda. It
was published in St. Petersburg in 1901. This book marks
a transitional period in Berdyaev's development during
which he was moving from Marxism to idealism.

Upon his return from his three-year-long exile in 1901,
the twenty-seven-year-old Berdyaev encountered Sergius
Bulgakov (1871–1944) who ignited a religious interest in
his heart. Bulgakov had previously been also a Marxist and
had taught economics in Kiev. Now he was turning with
profound interest and enthusiasm to Orthodoxy. A life-
time friendship developed between Berdyaev and Bulgakov, who later became the Dean of the Russian Theological Academy in Paris.

In 1903, Berdyaev went to Germany, where he studied
for a semester at the University of Heidelberg under Professor Wilhelm Windelband. Upon his return to Russia,
he met and married Lydia Yudifovna, and then settled in
St. Petersburg, where for two years he edited *The New
Way*. This journal, originally devoted to literary topics,

[2] Berdyaev, *Dream and Reality*, p. 18

had been in existence for three years when Berdyaev arrived in St. Petersburg. He and Bulgakov, as co-editors, attempted to make it an organ of political and philosophical ideas as well. In 1907, Berdyaev spent a few months in Paris, where he familiarized himself with contemporary religious and philosophical movements. When he returned to Russia, he relocated in Moscow, joining the Religious Philosophical Society there. (Founded to honor the memory of Vladimir Solovyev, this society brought together a diversified group of outstanding thinkers who discussed religious and artistic questions and ideas for political and social reform. Through Berdyaev's influence, a similar group was later formed in St. Petersburg.) Shortly before the Berdyaevs established themselves in Moscow, they made a visit to Italy.

The fourteen years spent in Moscow were a vital period in Berdyaev's life. Here the intellectual atmosphere was less agitated than in St. Petersburg, and the cultural milieu was broader and deeper. His friend Bulgakov, who himself had moved to Moscow, introduced him to a circle of religious thinkers who had experienced spiritual struggles similar to Berdyaev's own. Their open discussions of religious philosophy won his participation and aroused in him a new interest in the philosophy of Russian orthodoxy. His own philosophical ideas began to take a definite form and direction. In his religious life, he reached a positive decision and became a believing Christian. For a time he frequented the regular meetings of a group called "seekers after God," who represented one of the popular trends of the time, a mystical anarchism; however, he soon gave up this association because he was dissatisfied with their superficial attitude toward freedom. In the early years of this Moscow period, Berdyaev published two books, *The Philosophy of Freedom* (1911) and *A. S. Komyakov* (1912). An article entitled "Extinguishers of the Spirit" which he wrote in 1914 criticizing the Holy

2*

Governing Synod resulted in his being tried before a civil court. However, with the outbreak of the First World War, the court's interest waned; the trial dragged through the war years and was finally given up when the Communist Revolution broke out in 1917.

The later years of Berdyaev's Moscow period saw a tremendous literary output and a daring struggle for freedom. *The Spirit of Russia* appeared in 1915 and *The Meaning of the Creative Act* in 1916. In 1918 Berdyaev founded the Free Academy of Spiritual Culture, where courses in various subjects, seminars, and public lectures on controversial issues were given. The Academy at first enjoyed semi-official status, but government hostility gradually increased to the point where public announcements about its activities were prohibited and Berdyaev was prevented from publishing the books that grew out of his lectures. When he left the country in 1922, the Academy ceased to exist. Also in 1918 there appeared *The Destiny of Russia*, the last of Berdyaev's books to be published in Russia. In 1920 he was appointed to the chair of philosophy at the University of Moscow, which he held for only one year.

The World War and the 1917 Russian Revolution had a profound impact on Berdyaev, vividly and unforgettably impressing upon him how individual freedom and human personality were crushed by the blind forces of history. In *The Destiny of Russia*, he expressed his faith in his homeland and his love for his countrymen. At the same time, he registered his protest against the Soviet regime by writing *The Philosophy of Inequality*, although this book could not be published until after his arrival in Berlin four years later. Also in the few years before his banishment from Russia, Berdyaev wrote *The Meaning of History* and *Dostoyevsky*, both of which had to await publication until he was out of the country.

In the few years following the Revolution and preceding his permanent exile, Berdyaev fought Communism

chiefly on spiritual grounds. His sense of freedom deep-
ened and matured in the heat of the battle for liberation.
He gained firsthand experience of what Dostoyevsky
meant by the Legend of the Grand Inquisitor. He saw how
the masses traded their freedom for bread. But can man
live by bread alone? Dostoyevsky was right! Freedom is a
burden of which many would rather be relieved. But as
soon as they surrender their freedom and barter it away
for security, they cease to be human. This Berdyaev found
to be tragically true.

During those last few years in Russia, Berdyaev realized
in a large measure what it meant and what it cost to be
free. He also experienced what it meant to be under the
sway of economic necessity. Until the war, he had de-
pended on the income of an estate in Poland. Now he had
to earn his living as a writer in times when men were
hungry for bread, and through articles in which he attacked
the existing regime. A six-weeks imprisonment intensified
his longing for freedom. It was about this time that Berdyaev insisted in *Dostoyevsky* that "Revolution is mad-
ness, an obsession that attacks the personality, paralyses its
freedom, and subjects it completely to an impersonal and
unhuman force."[3]

Protesting against the Communist government in private and in public, Berdyaev knew only too well that it
would come to a choice between freedom and his homeland. He chose the former and was permanently expelled
from Russia in 1922. What he wrote about the "Slavery
of Revolution" in his book *Slavery and Freedom* seven-
teen years later was the crystallization of his own personal
experience:

> The destined fate of the revolution is that it inevitably
> leads to Terror and Terror is the loss of freedom, the loss of

[3] Berdyaev, *Dostoyevsky* (Prague, 1923), trans. by Donald
Attwater (New York: Sheed & Ward, 1934), p. 151

everybody's freedom, the loss of freedom for all. At the outset
revolution is pure and singleminded; it proclaims freedom, but
as the development of its immanent forces goes on, in the
power of the fateful dialectic which takes place in it, freedom
disappears and the reign of terror begins.[4]

Berdyaev spent two years in Berlin, during which he
became the dean of the newly founded Russian Scientific
Institute, lecturing also on ethics and Russian philosophy. He was instrumental in establishing the Religious-
Philosophical Academy, to which he devoted much time
and interest, and of which he became president. In Berlin
he made the acquaintance of Count Keyserling, who was
influential in the publication of a German translation of
The Meaning of History and wrote a preface to it. Here
also Berdyaev met Max Scheler and Oswald Spengler.
During this period his prophetic inclinations found expression in *The New Middle Ages* (1923). This little book
proved to be a beacon which attracted the attention of
thinkers throughout the world. In it Berdyaev showed how
man had entered the Renaissance with the spiritual resources developed in the Middle Ages, but how his trust
in himself and in his scientific achievements led him to his
modern predicament. He also called on the West to oppose the forces of evil and to make Christianity the foundation of culture and civilization.

It was in Paris, to which he moved in 1924, that Berdyaev "came to share the life of the West fully."[5] The
Berdyaevs never had children, but their family had grown
to three while they were living in Moscow, when Berdyaev's sister-in-law, Eugenie, joined them permanently.
The three with Berdyaev's pet cat, Muri, settled in Cla-
mart outside the French capital. In his autobiography,
Berdyaev mentions a few of the "many reasons for moving

[4] Berdyaev, *Slavery and Freedom*, p. 195
[5] Berdyaev, *Dream and Reality*, p. 250

to France."[6] He had been intending to settle in France ever since his departure from Russia. Paris was replacing Berlin as the center of Russian life abroad. The Religious-Philosophical Academy had also been transferred to Paris. Because of his half-French upbringing, Berdyaev naturally felt more at home in France.

In the West Berdyaev found the freedom to develop his philosophy of freedom. In the course of the next fifteen years, he published a total of nine books. He founded a religious-philosophical review, the monthly journal *Put'* (The Way), which became the voice of Russian religious philosophy and which he continued to edit until the outbreak of World War II. In Paris he met and associated with Jacques Maritain and Gabriel Marcel as well as many of his former friends such as Bulgakov, who was now the dean of the newly founded Russian Theological Academy. In 1939 he was invited to lecture at the Sorbonne. The revised French edition of his *Freedom and the Spirit* won an award from the French Academy. In 1947 Cambridge University conferred on him the honorary degree of Doctor of Divinity. The same year he was invited to be one of the speakers at an international meeting in Switzerland at which the subject "Technical Progress and Moral Progress" was discussed.

Berdyaev did not encounter extreme difficulties or danger to his life during the German occupation of France in the Second World War. He was visited and questioned by the Gestapo a number of times, but that was all. The war and postwar years were for him a time of enormous literary output. He saw the publication of *The Russian Idea* (1946), *The Beginning and the End* (Russian title: *An Essay in Eschatological Metaphysics*, 1947), and *The Divine and the Human* (1947). Three other volumes, *Dream and Reality* (Russian title: *Self-Knowledge, An Essay in*

[6] *Ibid.*, p. 253

Philosophical Autobiography, 1949), *The Realm of Spirit and the Realm of Caesar* (1949), and *Truth and Revelation* (1953) were published after his sudden death in 1948, three years following that of his wife.

2   HISTORICAL FACTORS

Berdyaev's loyalty to Russia was never broken. His permanent exile did not change his love for the land and its people. His life continued to be a part of Russia, and Russia continued to be a part of him. His identification with its destiny was unequivocal; whatever happened to Russia was simultaneously happening to him. Referring to the 1917 Communist Revolution, Berdyaev wrote:

> The Revolution did not take place only outside and beyond me, an event having no common measure with my own life and so without any meaning for me; it was also as it were an interior happening within me. Bolshevism has been embodied in Russia and triumphed there because *I* am what *I am*, because there was no real spiritual power in me, none of the strength of faith that can move mountains; it was my sin, and an affliction that is visited on me.[7]

The Russian landscape, Russian history, the Russian people and their culture all had their part in shaping Berdyaev's intellectual and spiritual life. The immense vastness of the Russian land must have left a deep imprint on his thinking. The absence of natural limits so characteristic of the plains and steppes in Russia no doubt played a role in creating its counterpart within him, a Russian soul expressed in a temperament reluctant to recognize any boundaries, a spirit with a deep passion for freedom. In *The Russian Idea*, he wrote:

> There is that in the Russian soul which corresponds to the

[7] Berdyaev, *The End of our Time*, trans. by Donald Attwater (New York: Sheed & Ward, 1933), p. 134

immensity, the vagueness, the infinitude of the Russian land,. spiritual geography corresponds with physical.[8]

Berdyaev saw very clearly both the dark and the bright sides of Russia's historical destiny. The fate of the Russian people in history, he repeatedly wrote, has been an unhappy one, full of suffering. But some of this suffering is an inevitable part of the messianic mission of the Russian people. The vocation of "Holy Russia," Berdyaev firmly believed, "is above all else bound up with the social transformation of the world."[9] This is what he meant by "the Russian Idea," an idealized Russia that would put an end to imperialistic nationalism and become the advocate of universalism. "The Russian Idea includes the synthesis of East and West, of two cultures in world history."[10] Berdyaev discussed this prophetic theme at some length in his work, *The Russian Idea*. In *Toward a New Epoch*, he sums up this world role of Russia when he writes:

> The historic destiny of the Russian people is to create a social order more just and more human than that of the West. It has to realize the brotherhood of men and of peoples, for that *is* the Russian Idea.[11]

But it was impossible for Berdyaev to find an organic unity in Russian history. The Kiev period, in spite of its promising achievements, came to a catastrophic end. Two centuries under foreign rule followed. The Russia of the Moscow period attained military strength, but its intellectual culture remained weak. Russian boundaries were expanded, but the Russian soul was depressed. The last decades of this Moscow period marked the beginning of

[8] Berdyaev, *The Russian Idea*, trans. by R. M. French (New York: The Macmillan Co., 1948), p. 2

[9] Berdyaev, *Toward a New Epoch*, trans. by Oliver Fielding Clarke (London: Geoffrey Bles, 1949), p. 69

[10] *Ibid.*

[11] Op. cit. p. 67

the split in the Russian soul, as the Orthodox Church bowed before Moscow's growing political and military power. On the surface, church and state looked neatly welded together, but it was an artificial and short-lived compromise. The Russian people felt this and it caused them much inner suffering. "The Russian Idea," that is, "the idea of community and brotherhood of men and peoples,"[12] could not possibly find its realization in the Moscow period. Thus the destiny of the Russian people, the creation of a world-wide brotherhood with the formation of a Christian society, was denied fulfillment by both the state and the church. In Berdyaev's opinion, this was a betrayal of the Russian people.

The Reform of Peter the Great (1672–1725) was unavoidable, but it was achieved by force and did violence to the soul of the people and to their beliefs. Peter was "a revolutionary from above," as Berdyaev puts it, who brought about the subjection of the church to the state. His empire grew outwardly but shrank inwardly, lacking an inner unity. The bulk of the Russian people lived in serfdom, able to endure suffering through their Orthodox faith.

In brief, the history of Russia abounds with tragedies. During the nineteenth and twentieth centuries, the country has been exposed to a number of invasions from the West; and between 1905 and 1917, it was rent by several revolutions, the last followed by civil war. Berdyaev never failed to feel himself a part of his people and a participant in their destiny. Their sufferings were his sufferings, their struggle for freedom was his struggle, and their hopes for a better future were also his hopes. Reacting to the Nazi regime's attack upon his homeland when he himself was living in France, Berdyaev wrote later on in his autobiography:

[12] Berdyaev, *The Russian Idea*, p. 254

The invasion of the Russian land by the German armies
shook me to the depth of my being. I felt that *my* Russia was
exposed to mortal danger, that she might be dismembered and
enslaved.[13]

This intimate and sincere identification with the history
and destiny of the Russian people gives an existential
flavor to Berdyaev's philosophy of freedom. His greatness
lies partly in his realistic perspective on the historical process, which enabled him to see the inevitability of the
Russian Revolution and Soviet rule, and partly in his prophetic vision, which led him to insist in the name of freedom that the present state of historical development is
transitional and must be followed by a new and brighter
era of Russian history. As a realist, Berdyaev saw in the
revolution a judgment upon the old regime and the church
that became its tool.[14] In the light of his philosophy of
history, he could very well understand why certain freedoms must be restricted by revolutions, and why there
was no place for him in Russia. Nevertheless, he never
lost faith in Russia and foresaw the time when freedom
would return to his native land: "freedom to breathe, to
think, to move about, to stop at home, to live a spiritual
life."[15] It was his fervent hope that when the social problems had been ironed out the religious vocation of the
Russian people would assert itself and realize its goal of
world-wide fraternity.

3   RELIGIOUS IMPACT

Berdyaev was the son of the Orthodox Church, in whose
full communion he remained all his life.[16] No doubt, the
ruling principle of the church's polity, the "belief that

13 Berdyaev, *Dream and Reality*, p. 317
14 Berdyaev, *The End of our Time*, p. 163 f
15 *Ibid.*, p. 133
16 Berdyaev, *Dream and Reality*, p. 177

each nation should form its own church, and that all these national units should enjoy equality and freedom within the great family of the Eastern Orthodox,"[17] appealed to him. The constitution of the Eastern Orthodox Church is built on the fundamental principle of self-government in which both clergy and laity share. This implies a very close link between the Orthodox Church and the culture and history of the land to which it belongs. In this sense, Orthodoxy is national, and it was the emphasis on autonomy that made the Orthodox Church the first to resist the claims of the Papacy. Nevertheless, the quality of its faith and the uniformity of its worship makes it international as well. There is a complete unity of doctrine and discipline which transcends the national border.

Furthermore, there is a simplicity and freedom in Orthodox theology that must have impressed Berdyaev, leaving its effect upon his philosophy of freedom. The Orthodox Church experienced no Reformation and Counter-Reformation and, consequently, escaped the necessity of redefining and overdefining its theological terms and recasting its dogmas in rigid doctrinal forms.[18] This means that there is more theological elbow-room in Orthodoxy than is the case in Protestantism or Catholicism. It means a greater measure of freedom of thought. For Berdyaev, these qualities were highly significant.[19] He felt at home in the Orthodox Church particularly because of its non-authoritarian attitude and practices. "I have not known authority . . . , most particularly, in my religious life."[20] Authority in matters of Christian truth is vested in the minds and hearts of the people who constitute the Orthodox Church, and that by virtue of the indwelling Spirit of

[17] Nicolas Zernov, *The Church of the Eastern Christians* (New York: The Macmillan Co., 1944), p. 16

[18] Sergius Bulgakov, *The Orthodox Church* (New York: 1935), Chapter VI

[19] Berdyaev, *Dream and Reality*, p. 177

[20] *Ibid.*, p. 48

God.[21] In this area of "democratic" freedom in the Orthodox Church, it was Alexey S. Khomyakov (1804–60), a layman, whose idea of freedom as the foundation of Christianity made a deep impression on Berdyaev.[22]

Khomyakov's contribution to Russian theological thought lies primarily in his delineation of the concept *sobornost*, which is the keystone of his ecclesiology with its teaching about freedom in the Orthodox Church and the rejection of external authority in Christian life. According to philologists, the word *sobornost* contains a wealth of connotations which renders it untranslatable into any Western European language. The term suggests "the idea of all-togetherness, of congregationalism, of catholicism as a spirit in which all work together creatively and to which all contribute."[23] "*Sobornost* suggests freedom and unity in love, a combination of liberty and order which results from the indwelling of Christ by the Holy Spirit in those who are baptized."[24] According to Nicolas Zernov, the term *sobornost*, by which the Church is described, "denotes for the Orthodox *togetherness*, unity in freedom, the victory of harmony over chaos, and of love over hatred and fear."[25] Berdyaev discusses the meaning of *sobornost* in Chapter VII of his book *The Realm of Spirit and the Realm of Caesar* as the very contrary of collectivism and as a concept that has more in common with the word community. "Community and sobornost always recognize freedom and the value of the person."[26]

[21] Bulgakov, *The Orthodox Church*, Chapter II

[22] Berdyaev, *Dream and Reality*, p. 165 (Berdyaev wrote a book on Khomyakov which was published in 1912)

[23] Evgueny Lampert, *Nicolas Berdyaev and the New Middle Ages* (London: James Clark & Co., 1945), p. 19

[24] O. Fielding Clarke, *Introduction to Berdyaev* (London: Geoffrey Bles, 1950), p. 23

[25] Zernov, *The Church of the Eastern Christians*, p. 64

[26] Berdyaev, *The Realm of Spirit and the Realm of Caesar*, p. 123

Some significant aspects and implications of *sobornost*
find clear expression in Orthodox worship itself where
form and freedom are combined. Noteworthy is the fact
that the pulpit, which represents authority, is, as a rule,
absent in Orthodox churches. During the greater part of
the service, the altar and the priests are not seen by the
congregation, remaining concealed behind the screen with
three doors that divides the chancel and the nave. The
altar is seen only when the middle door is opened. The
worship itself is characterized by considerable freedom
and spontaneous action.[27]

The absence of regimentation and constraints in Orthodox worship and the remarkable combination of order
and freedom must have left their mark on Berdyaev's
personality. Berdyaev took his religion seriously in spite of
his dissatisfaction and often loudly expressed criticisms at
many corruptions in church life and administration. Both
his mind and heart responded to Orthodoxy. His philosophical inquiries and metaphysical excursions did not
hamper his actual participation in worship with his fellow church members. "The matter of religion," Berdyaev
writes, "has never failed to exercise my mind and heart."[28]

4   LITERARY STIMULATION

Berdyaev was keenly aware of his Russian heritage. In
Dream and Reality, he frankly and appreciatively states
his affinity to the past and gives grateful recognition to all
his intellectual and spiritual ancestors.[29]

He had deep sympathy with the Slavophiles who turned
their attention to the East, to Russia itself, and insisted
that in its traditions and institutions, in its soil and air,
Russia had the adequate resources for its own spiritual

27 Zernov, *The Church of the Eastern Christians*, p. 27
28 Berdyaev, *Dream and Reality*, p. 170
29 *Ibid.*, p. xiv

and intellectual development. The Slavophiles were also warm defenders of personal freedom, the freedom of conscience, thought and speech. The greatest name among the early Slavophiles was Khomyakov, mentioned above, who saw in history the conflict of two principles: freedom and necessity, spirituality and materialism.[30] He fought against necessity, the power of the material over the spiritual, all his life. For him freedom was the highest of all values. Khomyakov saw the power of necessity suppressing freedom in paganism, Roman Catholicism, Western rationalism and especially in Hegel's philosophy. He paid due reverence to the freely creative spirit.

Berdyaev also acknowledged the fact that he received a profound impression from the Westernizers who looked to the West for intellectual leadership. He felt very indebted to Alexander Herzen (1812–70), one of the most freedom-loving of Russians. Herzen engaged in "an ardent defence of freedom."[31] He directed his ideological warfare against Hegel's philosophy of history, in which human personality is crushed by the world spirit and by progress. He vigorously objected to the sacrifice of human personality to history and to its conversion into an instrument for the attainment of inhuman ends. He would not consent "to sacrifice present generations for the sake of generations to come."[32]

Another passionate lover of freedom who was a source of inspiration to Berdyaev was the great Russian poet, A. S. Pushkin (1799–1837). "Without Pushkin," Berdyaev claims, "Dostoyevsky and Tolstoy would have been impossible."[33] Pushkin, whom Berdyaev called "the real

[30] V. V. Zenkovsky, A *History of Russian Philosophy*, trans. by George L. Kline (New York: Columbia University Press; London: Routledge & Kegan Paul Ltd., 1953), Vol. I, p. 189

[31] *Ibid.*, p. 298

[32] Berdyaev, *The Russian Idea*, p. 64

[33] *Ibid.*, p. 63

singer of freedom,"[34] combined his love for it with a love
for the greatness of Russia. But he also lamented the lack
of freedom in Russia and entertained universal aspirations
for his freedom, as the lines from his poem on "Freedom"
indicate:

> I sing the freedom of the world
> And smite the vice on kingly throne.[35]

The literary-philosophical writers who provided Berdyaev with the largest measure of intellectual stimulation
and spiritual inspiration were Leo Tolstoy (1828–1910)
and Fyodor Dostoyevsky (1821–81). Berdyaev speaks
quite frequently of his indebtedness to them, particularly
in understanding the nature of man.[36]

Tolstoy, who had the lesser influence of the two on
Berdyaev, was haunted by the meaninglessness of civilized
life with all its artificialities and falsities. He attacked the
confinements that political, social, and religious institutions impose upon people. His disgust with civilization
and sympathetic love of the less fortunate among men is
expressed in his account of an experience he had in Lu-
cerne. An itinerant Tyrolean was singing in the town
square. All people around him enjoyed his singing and
were deeply touched by it. However, they all turned away
laughingly the moment the man began to take up a collec-
tion. Tolstoy, who was watching the scene, was sadly and
indignantly shaken by the reaction of so-called civilized
men.

I felt hurt, bitter and ashamed of the little man, of the
crowd and of myself . . . Why is it that this fact . . . is possi-

[34] Berdyaev, *The Origin of Russian Communism* (London:
Geoffrey Bles, 1937), p. 25
[35] *Ibid.*, p. 79
[36] Berdyaev, *Dream and Reality*, p. 83

ble here, where civilization, freedom and equality have reached the highest degree?[37]

It was Tolstoy who opened Berdyaev's eyes to the various forms that slavery assumes in Western civilization and thus intensified his eager search for freedom. In *Slavery and Freedom*, Berdyaev writes:

> Tolstoy's revolt against the false standards of greatness and the false sanctities of history, against the falsity of all social position and the social relations of mankind, penetrated my very being.[38]

But it must be pointed out that Tolstoy's influence on Berdyaev was informative rather than formative.[39] For Berdyaev, Tolstoy was too much of a nihilist who rejected past, traditions, old culture, state, and church. True, Tolstoy preached that life is essentially love, but he was a perfectionist in a fanatical way. Berdyaev could not accept Tolstoy's basic conviction that "man is only a part of the cosmic life and that he ought to be merged with nature which is divine."[40] Tolstoy was mainly interested in things as they were, in that which is. Berdyaev, on the other hand, was more interested in that which is to be. And in this he had more affinity with, and received a greater impetus from, Dostoyevsky.[41] It may be said that Tolstoy's influence on Berdyaev consisted chiefly in the artistic portrayal of the negative and static aspects of things as they exist. Berdyaev benefited a great deal from Tolstoy's accomplished literary paintings of slavery in its different dresses and disguises. The impact of Dostoyevsky on Berdyaev's

[37] V. V. Zenkovsky, *Russian Thinkers and Europe*, trans. by G. S. Bodde (Ann Arbor, Michigan: J. W. Edward Publisher), p. 121

[38] Berdyaev, *Slavery and Freedom*, p. 12

[39] Berdyaev, *Dream and Reality*, p. 111

[40] Berdyaev, *The Russian Idea*, p. 181

[41] Berdyaev, *Dream and Reality*, p. 49

life and thought was more positive. It was definitely in the
arena of freedom. Berdyaev stood early in life at the gate
of that arena, and Dostoyevsky played a vital role in luring
him in.

In the Introduction of his book *Dostoyevsky*, Berdyaev
begins with this testimony:

> Dostoyevsky has played a decisive part in my spiritual life.
> While I was still a youth a slip from him, so to say, was grafted
> upon me. He stirred and lifted up my soul more than any
> other writer or philosopher has done.[42]

Dostoyevsky was a passionate advocate of freedom. The
problem of freedom is central in his writings. It troubled
his mind more than anything else. He conceived of freedom not as a right of man but as an obligation, a duty.
As such, freedom is a burden. Furthermore, the question
of freedom in Dostoyevsky is inescapably linked to the
problem of suffering. Freedom, which is the fruit of man's
likeness to God, and the indication of his inalienable dignity, very easily passes into willfulness, and willfulness
generates evil, and evil begets suffering. It is here in these
turbulent waters that we come to the Dostoyevskyian
paradox: on the one hand, Dostoyevsky cannot accept a
world with unmerited suffering, and on the other hand,
he cannot accept a world without conflict and suffering. In
other words, he does not want a world without freedom,
and yet, it is the very freedom that he advocates which
leads to suffering. His thought is expressed in Ivan Karamazov's statement in *The Brothers Karamazov*: "I absolutely repudiate the highest harmony; it is not worth the
tears of this one tormented child."

The whole problem of freedom and its related problems
of suffering and happiness are all summed up in Dostoyevsky's great chapter of *The Brothers Karamazov*, "The Leg-

[42] Berdyaev, *Dostoyevsky*, p. 7

end of the Grand Inquisitor," which, in Berdyaev's estimate, is "the summit of Dostoyevsky's creation."[43]
Berdyaev seems literally haunted by this legend. In most
of his writings, he turns back to the story over and over
again. In the Legend of the Grand Inquisitor, Dostoyevsky
diagnoses the basic problem of Christianity and the tragedy of mankind. The Grand Inquisitor takes as his starting point the belief that humanity is not suited for Christian freedom. He accuses Christ of not really loving man,
because otherwise He would not have burdened him with
freedom. The Grand Inquisitor himself claims to reverse
Christ's action. He knows that the burden of freedom is
beyond the strength of man, and, therefore, he proposes
to bequeath to man true happiness by relieving him of his
burden of freedom, by taking from him the freedom of
determining the course of his action.

The Grand Inquisitor is a personification of the dangerous idea that Christ's redeeming work can be consummated only after humanity has been coerced into submission to a single ecclesiastical authority. Dostoyevsky firmly
believed that the chaos and amoralism in which mankind
finds itself is a by-product of its rejection of Christ's teachings of true freedom. European culture is contaminated
because it is void of Christian freedom. Christ's teachings
have been replaced by human teachings. In Dostoyevsky's
view, the very core of Christ's Gospel has been perverted
and His good news about freedom has been rejected. People have been forced into what is believed to be a social
paradise but at the expense of their freedom.

Dostoyevsky prophetically foresaw the socialist dictator-
ships that would be guided by the spirit of the Grand
Inquisitor in achieving the greatest happiness for the
greatest number but at the expense of freedom. He firmly
believed that man does not live by bread alone. He would

[43] Berdyaev, *The Russian Idea*, p. 180

not relieve man of the burden of his freedom, and would not exempt him from suffering at the price of his liberty.

He felt the rightness and inevitability of this paradox with deep conviction and strong passion. He studied the destiny of man from the point of view of his freedom and found that if man is deprived of his freedom, sooner or later he will rebel and expose himself to hardships of all sorts in order to regain it. But Dostoyevsky did not overlook the difficulties generated by freedom in a naturalistic order of life, that is, in a life without Christ. Freedom is irrational. It can create both good and evil. Throughout his novels, Dostoyevsky shows how freedom degenerates into arbitrary self-will, and how this leads to evil, and the result is suffering. But suffering, according to Dostoyevsky, is redemptive. Life is the expiation of sin through suffering by which the lost freedom is recovered. Without freedom, man ceases to be man. But the path of freedom is the path of suffering too, and man must follow it to the end.

Much of the form and content of Berdyaev's concept of freedom was supplied by Dostoyevsky. In the Dostoyevskyian dialectic, Berdyaev found the main outline not only of the problem of freedom but also of its solution. In the Legend of the Grand Inquisitor, he saw the intricacies of freedom exposed and its real nature revealed. Every man is offered and must choose between the two alternatives: that of the Grand Inquisitor, the principle of compulsion, or that of Christ, the principle of freedom. Christ's overcoming the three temptations, the possibility of winning man's allegiance by bread, by an earthly kingdom or by miracles, was a victory of the principle of freedom over the principle of compulsion. Unfortunately, many people choose the principle of coercion and thus, in the name of human happiness and personal contentment, renounce freedom.

Dostoyevsky identified the image of Christ with the

spirit of freedom. Christ appeals to the free spirit of man. He does not force man into obedience. He made freedom possible by rejecting all temporal authority for himself. He knew no power except that of love, which is alone compatible with freedom. Dostoyevsky makes the Grand Inquisitor say to Christ:

> The freedom of their faith was dearer to thee than anything . . . Thou didst desire man's free love . . . Man must freely decide for himself what is good and what is evil, having only thine image before him as a guide instead of the rigid law of old.

At the basis of Dostoyevsky's exaltation of human freedom lies his high regard for the human personality, which is found in all men and is inalienable. The stress he laid on the independence and dignity of the human personality led him to distinguish between two kinds of freedom: an initial freedom and a final freedom. The Truth shall make men free—this is the final freedom; but man must freely accept the Truth—this is the initial freedom. Christ gives man the final liberty which is accepted by man freely, that is, through the initial freedom that he already possesses.

Dostoyevsky may be regarded as the spiritual godfather of Berdyaev, who wrote of him: "I personally know no more profoundly Christian writer than Dostoyevsky,"[44] and "So great is the worth of Dostoyevsky that to have produced him is by itself sufficient justification for the existence of the Russian people in the world."[45]

5 PHILOSOPHICAL ROOTS

a. *Vladimir Solovyev* Berdyaev often referred to Vladimir Solovyev (1853–1900) as one of those by whom he was influenced. He regarded this mystical and poetical

[44] Berdyaev, *Dostoyevsky*, p. 209
[45] *Ibid.*, p. 227

philosopher as the greatest of Russian thinkers of the
nineteenth century. Before discussing Solovyev's influence
on Berdyaev, it seems pertinent to state the general characteristics of Russian philosophy, which gave a definite
color and direction to the thinking of both.

Russian philosophy has shown little interest in the theory of knowledge as a central philosophical discipline. It
has tended to give expression to individual spiritual needs.
In the words of V. V. Zenkovsky (1881–1962), professor
of philosophy at the Russian Orthodox Institute in Paris
1926–62, "Russian thought remained at all times con-
nected with its own religious elementality, its own religious soil."[46] This meant a sustained preoccupation, above
all, with man, his fate, his freedom and the meaning of
his life.[47] Out of this anthropocentric emphasis of Russian philosophy grew an excessive interest in the philosophy of history as well as in ethical issues and political and
social problems.[48] Another important quality of Russian
thought, largely due to its close association with Orthodoxy, is that it tends to be intensely mystical.[49] To sum
up, one could say that the ethical and mystical qualities
are dominant in Russian philosophy and render it fundamentally a philosophy of religion with genuine concern
for its social, economic, and political implications and ap-
plications. This is particularly true of the philosophies of
both Solovyev and Berdyaev.

In many aspects of his philosophy, which is syncretistic
rather than original, Solovyev is preoccupied with the
problem of freedom. He is particularly concerned with the

[46] Zenkovsky, A History of Russian Philosophy, Vol. I, p. 2
[47] Ibid., p. 6
[48] Ibid., p. 6; Cf. Thomas G. Masaryk, The Spirit of Russia:
Studies in History, Literature and Philosophy, trans. by Eden and
Cedar Paul (New York: The Macmillan Co., 1919), pp. 199–201
[49] Masaryk, The Spirit of Russia: Studies in History, Literature and Philosophy, p. 199 ff

attainment of liberation from the domination of the natural forces within himself and around him. He considers liberty and equality to be the two inalienable rights of man:

> If the supreme value of man as such, his status of being a law unto himself, is recognized, then the acknowledgment of his freedom follows naturally: for nothing can have power over him who is himself the source of all power; and, as the status of man belongs to all people, (their) equality follows from the same (premise).[50]

Solovyev's analysis of the nature of freedom is penetrating and seems to have left a lasting impression on Berdyaev's thinking. He thought that the idea of necessity, taken in a broad sense, does not by any means exclude freedom. "Freedom is but one of the species of necessity," Solovyev radically asserts, and "when freedom is contrasted with necessity," he continues, "this contrast usually signifies the contrast between the internal and the external necessity."[51]

At another point in his *Lectures on God-manhood*, Solovyev identifies "true freedom" with "internal necessity."[52] Illustrating this seemingly contradictory statement, he says, for instance, "it is necessary for God to love all and to manifest the eternal idea of the good in (all) creation."[53] He explains this in the following manner:

> God cannot nourish enmity, in God there can be no hatred: love, reason, freedom, are necessary with God. We must say (in other words) that for God freedom is necessary—which in-

[50] Vladimir Solovyev, *Lectures on God-manhood*, Lecture I, trans. by Peter P. Zouboff (with Introduction) in *Godmanhood as the Main Idea of the Philosophy of Vladimir Solovyev* (New York: Harmon Printing House, 1944), p. 80

[51] *Ibid.*, Lecture I, p. 87

[52] *Ibid.*, Lecture VI, p. 138

[53] *Ibid.*, Lecture II, p. 96

dicates that freedom cannot be a concept logically, unconditionally excluding the concept of necessity.[54]

Solovyev reveals his affinity to Jacob Boehme (see below) when he talks about *the unconditional beginning, the unconditional central principle.* He conceives of religion as the reunion of man and the world with this unconditional and integral principle which is God, the Absolute. Salvation is the realization of true equality, freedom, and brotherhood. The Church represents the unconditional divine beginning and, therefore, everything else must be conditional and dependent on it for its union with the Absolute.[55]

Apparently the unconditional beginning, the central principle or, simply, the divine beginning of Solovyev was transformed by Berdyaev into the concept of *uncreated freedom.* The same idea is expressed by Boehme in the *Ungrund.* For Solovyev, the divine beginning, which is free from all being and from all determination, is at the same time and thereby the positive force and power of all being. In that sense, the divine beginning itself is *all.*[56]

Solovyev's concept of *Godmanhood* (Bogochelovechestve) and what it means to the human personality has also had an impact on Berdyaev's thinking. According to Solovyev, man is the uniting link between the divine and the natural world. He combines in himself all opposites, which can be reduced to one great polarity between the unconditional and the conditioned, between the absolute and eternal essence, on the one hand, and the transitory phenomenon or appearance, on the other. Man is at once divinity and nothingness. Solovyev equates faith in human personality and faith in God; for divinity belongs not only

[54] Vladimir Solovyev, *Lectures on God-manhood,* Lecture II, p. 96
[55] *Ibid.,* Lecture I, p. 87
[56] *Ibid.,* Lecture IV, p. 119

to God but also to man: with this one difference, namely, that God possesses it in eternal reality, while man can only have it granted to him. In the given state of man, divinity is only a possibility, only an aspiration.[57] In the words of Berdyaev,

> The idea of Godmanhood means the overcoming of the self-sufficiency of man in humanism and at the same time the affirmation of the activity of man, of his highest dignity, of the divine in man.[58]

One more area in which Solovyev exercised an influence on Berdyaev must be mentioned: that of his universal outlook. Solovyev had a keen sense of history and a strong belief in the unity of history. Even the fundamental concept of his philosophy—Godmanhood or Divine-Humanity —developed as a basically historical concept. Both East and West are necessary for each other and for the spread of Christianity throughout the world.

Solovyev's universal outlook freed him from the provincialism of both the Slavophiles and the Westernizers. It is true, Solovyev's philosophy evoked no echo in Russia itself, but his Christian universalism as well as his great capacity for understanding of all epochs and all peoples are part of the rich heritage he left for mankind. He was one of the early pioneers of freedom, who devoted his efforts to the liberation of humanity from the evils of historical provincialism, and Berdyaev followed in his steps.

b. *Jacob Boehme*   Berdyaev was well aware of his philosophical kinship to Jacob Boehme (1575–1624) and of the impact this great mystic exercised on him. Referring to the years before the 1917 Revolution, he wrote:

> Already then I felt attracted to Jacob Boehme and his idea of *Ungrund*. Acquaintance with this greatest of all mystics

[57] *Ibid.*, Lecture II, p. 98
[58] Berdyaev, *The Russian Idea*, p. 173

has colored my approach to the problem of freedom ever since.[59]

Earlier in his autobiography, Berdyaev also points to this important root of his philosophical thinking: "The only conception of freedom which I found satisfactory was that of Jacob Boehme, whose writings I came to appreciate more and more."[60] At the time he was attracted by Boehme, Berdyaev had been searching for an ontological answer to the problem of freedom. He was not satisfied with the answer of the Eastern Orthodox Church that man received freedom from God when he was created. For Berdyaev, this view made God responsible for evil. In his effort to solve the problem and counteract the reformers who tried to solve it with the rationalization of predestination, he turned to Boehme in whose mysticism he found an ontological base on which his concept of freedom could safely stand.

In Boehme are strangely but uniquely mingled: primitive mysticism, Lutheran theology, medieval metaphysics, and a modern objective attitude toward man and nature. Despite his syncretism, Boehme was amazingly original. He was, so to speak, a philosophical chemist who was able to produce something totally new out of well-known substances. He loved nature as a scientist and loved God as a Christian and the two he tried to unite. In the words of Windelband, "the deep earnestness of the religious need which lay at the basis of the German Reformation did not allow him to content himself with the separation of religious metaphysics and natural science, customary at his time, and he sought to work the two into one again."[61] In a way, Boehme attempted to reconcile the other-

[59] Berdyaev, *Dream and Reality*, p. 179

[60] *Ibid.*, p. 99

[61] Wilhelm Windelband, A *History of Philosophy*, trans. by James H. Tufts (New York: The Macmillan Co., 1901), p. 374

worldly attitude of the Middle Ages and the this-worldly emphasis of the Renaissance. For him, as Howard Brinton put it, the problem was to bring about a "union between the in-going will toward the Oneness of God and the out-going will toward the many of nature."[62] Thus Boehme sought to harmonize the ancient contrast between the opposites, the One and the Many, the Absolute and the Relative, the Universal and the Particular.

In his attempt to reach a synthesis, Boehme mobilized his intellectual energies in an effort to understand, first of all, the essence of the Absolute represented by the biblical God of creation. This he thought would be possible if God is conceived primarily as Will. In this he followed the tradition of Origen, Augustine, and Duns Scotus. Boehme tried to see through the mystery of the Divine Will which he identified with the Ultimate Principle. As Richard Kroner has pointed out, "he (Boehme) became thereby the first Christian philosopher to develop theosophic thoughts."[63]

What is the nature of the Divine Will? Boehme insisted that it cannot be compared with human will, which must constantly strive toward an objective because it lacks perfection. The Divine Will is omnipotent, omnipresent, free, and eternal. There is something in it, Boehme continues, that can be thought of only in terms of a bottomless, fathomless abyss. This *abysmal will* he called *Ungrund*, that is, without a basis. Yet it is at the basis of all things. Consisting of nothing, the *Ungrund* is an infinity, transcending everything else. It cannot be compared with anything and must, therefore, be called Nothing. Boehme often describes this *Ungrund* as a dark abyss that is pure and aimless Will. The *Ungrund* is absolutely groundless

[62] Howard H. Brinton, *The Mystic Will* (New York: The Macmillan Co., 1930), p. 43

[63] Richard Kroner, *Speculation and Revelation in Modern Philosophy* (Philadelphia: The Westminster Press, 1961), p. 69

in a sense that it has no motive or goal outside itself. It is
absolute free Will, determined by nothing outside itself.
"The *Ungrund* is an eternal Nothing but makes an eternal
beginning as a desire."[64] This "eternal Nothing," however, is at the same time the eternal *All*, the totality of
being. "This is the eye of the *Ungrund* . . . wherein all
lies whether it is in time or eternity."[65]

Boehme bases his argument for freedom on the assumption that the human will is also a Nothing which has its
origin in the primordial abyss, the *Ungrund*, that is the
source of all things, both good and evil. Boehme sometimes calls the *Ungrund* liberty. As such, it is free to
manifest itself. Through this self-manifestation or self-
articulation, the impersonal *Ungrund* becomes the personal Creator. A similar process, according to Boehme,
takes place in man's will, which is based on nothing but
itself. "The soul's free will, which also has its origin in the
abyss, conceives itself into something whereby it may become."[66] Again, "the will shapes its own form in the spirit;
it can give to the body another form out of the centre of
nature, for the inner is the lord of the outer."[67]

It may be said that Boehme's philosophy takes the form
of a theosophy in which a Will strives to know itself, starting at the lowest level as a blind force, as a formless and
fathomless abyss. Through its own desire, the Will develops an inner conflict and becomes the equivalent of

[64] Jacob Boehme, *Mysterium Pansophicum* (Vom himm-
lischen und irdischen Mysterio), 1:3; quoted and translated by
Howard H. Brinton, *The Mystic Will*, p. 109

[65] Boehme, *Mysterium Magnum*, 1:8; quoted and translated
by Howard H. Brinton, *The Mystic Will*, p. 194

[66] *Ibid.*, 27:6; quoted and translated by Brinton, *The Mystic
Will*, p. 107

[67] Boehme, *The Forty Questions* (Vierzig Fragen von der
Seele), 6:10; quoted and translated by Brinton, *The Mystic Will*,
p. 105

nature. Afterward it breaks through nature and appears
as the self-consciousness in man. Spiritual life is ignited in
man when the Will triumphs over nature. At this stage
of the Will's development, the divine Will appears as
the human will. The final goal of this development of the
Will is reached when a complete harmony between the
opposites, love and hate, joy and grief, is achieved. The
spiritual life is a continuous struggle which takes the form
of a mystic cycle in which the Divine Will manifests itself as the human will and the human will is transformed
into the Divine Will.

> God must become Man, man must become God, Heaven
> must be one with the earth and the earth must become Heaven.
> Wouldst thou make heaven out of the earth, then give the
> earth the food of heaven.[68]

> If thou willest to behold God and eternity, turn thy will
> around into thy inner self, then thou art like God himself, for
> so thou art created in the beginning and so thou livest in ac-
> cordance with the inner will of God and in God.[69]

Boehme's philosophical and theosophical ideas marked a
break with the intellectualism of the Greeks and Scholas-
tics. In his interpretation of cosmic life, Boehme to a certain extent anticipated Hegel through his stress on one
fundamental principle that underlies and unifies all that
exists. Brinton is right in his statement that "Boehme thus
attempted to do in the ethical and religious field what
Hegel attempted to do in the more inclusive epistemological field."[70] Boehme's dialectic, no doubt, was mystical

[68] Boehme, *Signatura Rerum* (Von der Geburt und Bezeich-
nung aller Wesen); quoted and translated by Brinton, *The Mystic
Will*, p. 241
[69] Boehme, *De triplici vita hominis* (Vom dreifachen Leben
des Menschen); quoted and translated by Kroner, *Speculation
and Revelation in Modern Philosophy*, p. 74
[70] Brinton, *The Mystic Will*, p. 257

rather than logical, closely linked to his own spiritual experience.

In an early period of his life, when he was searching for a solution of the problem of evil, Berdyaev was attracted by Boehme's mystical speculation. Boehme's philosophical thinking, particularly his theories that an irrational principle lies at the basis of being, that primordial freedom precedes being itself, and that freedom is uncreated and is derived from the *Ungrund,* seemed to meet Berdyaev's immediate philosophical needs.

> I do not claim to be true to Boehme in every respect, but I regarded his teaching concerning Ungrund as susceptible of my own interpretation, and I identified Ungrund with primordial freedom, which precedes all ontological determination.[71]

How far-reaching Boehme's influence on Berdyaev was, at least at one stage of his development, may in part be felt from the following quotation: "Freedom is not created by God: it is rooted in the Nothing, in the Ungrund . . . God the Creator cannot be held responsible for freedom which gave rise to evil."[72]

c. *Immanuel Kant* The molding effect which Immanuel Kant (1724–1804) had on Berdyaev is reflected in the many tributes that Berdyaev pays him:

> My true master in philosophy was Kant, and I have devoted most of my studies to his thought . . . Kant provided me with something that underlies my fundamental philosophical attitude.[73]

> As regards philosophical influence and ancestry, I am, as I have already said, increasingly aware of my kinship to Kant.[74]

[71] Berdyaev, *Dream and Reality,* p. 99
[72] Berdyaev, *The Destiny of Man,* p. 25
[73] Berdyaev, *Dream and Reality,* p. 93
[74] *Ibid.,* p. 101

He (Kant) was a metaphysician of freedom, even, it may be, the only metaphysician of freedom, and in this respect my attempt to set forth my own metaphysics of freedom will be derived from Kant.[75]

Berdyaev firmly believed that he stood right in the middle of the stream of freedom that flows from the high mountains of Kantian philosophy. It goes without saying, therefore, that in order to gain a better understanding of Berdyacv's philosophy of freedom, it is imperative that the concept of freedom in the philosophy of Kant be investigated.

For Kant, the will is supreme in human life. Man's willing is more fundamental than his knowing. His highest capacity and supreme duty lies in the actualization of his freedom in moral action. Ethical considerations, rather than speculative knowledge, come first in importance.

In the Kantian revolution, ethics replaces both physics and metaphysics. The Will is the sun around which the speculative planets rotate. By obeying the metaphysical law within his own will, man liberates himself from the realm of necessity imposed upon him by nature. As Richard Kroner puts it in his work, *Kant's Weltanschauung*, "By the subordination of the will to the moral law . . . man is able to free himself from the compulsion of natural necessity."[76] Moral action is the bridge on which man walks from necessity to freedom. The moral law, according to Kant, is man's dependable guide and competent liberator.

It was the vital contrast between nature and morality, between necessity and freedom, so fundamental in Kant's philosophy, which captivated Berdyaev's imagination and

[75] Berdyaev, *The Beginning and the End*, p. 8

[76] Richard Kroner, *Kant's Weltanschauung* (Tübingen: 1914), trans. by John E. Smith (Chicago: University of Chicago Press, 1956), p. 12

became the irresistible undercurrent of his philosophical thinking. According to Kant, man is the meeting place of two spheres: what is and what ought to be. As Dr. Kroner has shown, Kant's attempt to reconcile the dualism of nature and morality in some supersensible unity, in some ultimate subject, does not prove successful because "Kant intends to exalt the moral law as the summit of man's total existence, and yet he also wants to put God above this summit."[77] Thus the dualism must continue to exist as a moral necessity.

What left a lasting impression on Berdyaev was Kant's ethical subjectivism. Kant refers to man's birthright of freedom as "the one sole original, inborn right belonging to every man by virtue of his humanity."[78] But this inborn right to be free does not mean that freedom itself is a natural endowment. Kant insists that man is free because he ought to will and act as a free agent, a free subject. This is so because freedom belongs to the subject, which is a person. Freedom never belongs to the object, which is impersonal. In other words, man is the author of his own actions. He is not merely a product of nature but is also a moral agent who initiates his own deeds. For the sake of freedom, Kant restricts nature. It is through his power of self-determination that man is free. "Freedom in the practical sense is the independence of the will of coercion by sensuous impulses."[79] Man's power of self-determination, Kant asserts, is a cause that is radically distinct from the causes found in natural science in the world of physical phenomena. The cause in the former, namely,

[77] Richard Kroner, *Kant's Weltanschauung*, p. 46

[78] Immanuel Kant, *The Science of Right*, trans. by W. Hastie; in Vol. 42, *Great Books of the Western World* (Chicago: Encyclopaedia Britannica, 1952), p. 401

[79] Immanuel Kant, *Critique of Pure Reason*, trans. by J.M.D. Mieklejohn, Revised Edition (New York: Willey Book Co., 1943), p. 300

the will in rational beings and the ability of such will to operate without external causes, is itself freedom. On the other hand, the causes in the latter, that is, in irrational beings, are the working of physical necessity.[80]

As Wilhelm Windelband has pointed out, Kant's "categorical imperative must be the expression of the autonomy of the practical reason, i.e. of the pure self-determination of the rational will."[81] This means that freedom implies self-legislation. "What else then can freedom of the will be," Kant asks, "but autonomy, that is, the property of the will to be a law to itself?"[82] The rational will, according to Kant, being identical with pure practical reason, has the power to legislate for itself. The rational will is thus at one and the same time both originator and observer of the moral law. Legislating for itself, it obeys itself alone, "so that a free will and a will subject to moral laws are one and the same."[83]

In the words of Dr. Kroner, "No one before Kant had ever exalted man so much; no one had ever accorded him such a degree of metaphysical independence and self-dependence."[84] In Kantian philosophy, man is freed not only from nature but likewise from external supernatural powers. Man, therefore, is absolutely valuable in himself because his worth and dignity make him an end in himself and never a means. This worth, says Kant, belongs in the highest degree to the moral law itself. The motive which stimulates man to obey this law must be nothing but reverence for the law itself. The worth or dignity of

[80] Immanuel Kant, *Fundamental Principles of Metaphysics of Morals*, trans. by Thomas Kingsmill Abbot, Sixth Edition (London: Longmans, Green & Co., 1948), p. 65

[81] Windelband, A *History of Philosophy*, p. 553

[82] Kant, *Fundamental Principles of Metaphysics of Morals*, p. 65 f

[83] *Ibid.*, p. 66

[84] Kroner, *Kant's Weltanschauung*, p. 36 f

the moral law, however, passes over to the man who is determined by this alone in the whole extent of his experience, and is able to determine himself by the law itself, to be its agent, and to identify himself with it. Hence, as Windelband concludes,

> Reverence for the worth of man is for Kant the material principle of moral science. Man should do his duty not for the sake of advantage, but out of reverence for himself, and in his intercourse with his fellow-man he should make it his supreme maxim, never to treat him as mere means for the attainment of his own ends, but always to honor in him the worth of personality.[85]

Berdyaev did not accept the Kantian philosophy as a whole, as he himself tells us. He could not, for instance, accept Kant's analysis of the autonomy of personality. He rejected the definition of the value of personality in terms of its moral and rational nature.[86] Nevertheless, the revolutionizing philosophical influence of Kant on Berdyaev remains great. Speaking of certain ideas which in one form or another continued to be among his philosophical cargo, Berdyaev goes on to say:

> I feel a special affinity with the dualism of Kant, with his distinction between the realm of freedom and the realm of nature, with his doctrine of freedom as of a character which is apprehended by the mind, with the Kantian doctrine of the will, with his view of the world of phenomena as distinct from the real world.[87]

d. *Sören Kierkegaard* Sören Kierkegaard's (1813–55) name appears only a few times in Berdyaev's writings. On the surface, the influence of the "founder of Existentialism" on Berdyaev seems rather insignificant and hardly de-

---

[85] Windelband, *A History of Philosophy*, p. 555
[86] Berdyaev, *Slavery and Freedom*, p. 34
[87] *Ibid.*, p. 12

serves to be mentioned. Berdyaev reminds us that he was an existentialist before he began to read Kierkegaard's books.[88] He insists that neither Kierkegaard nor Heidegger nor Jaspers had any particular influence on him.[89]

Nevertheless, the effect which Kierkegaard's thinking had on Berdyaev was, in the opinion of this writer, greater than Berdyaev himself realized. In a few passages, Berdyaev gives expression to his affinity to Kierkegaard. He promptly responded to Kierkegaard's appeal against Hegelianism.[90] Referring to his duty to oppose the claims of legalistic morality, Berdyaev frankly states: "In this, as in some other respects, I took up the position of Kierkegaard."[91] By responding to Kierkegaard's call to fight Hegelianism, Berdyaev perhaps unwittingly was permitting Kierkegaard to be instrumental in the shaping of his own philosophy of freedom, particularly as it is related to the concepts of subjectivity, individuality, and personality.

Kierkegaard's philosophy was a reaction to Hegel's speculative system, which had reduced the individual to a mere link in the chain of the dialectical movement. In the gigantic Hegelian philosophic structure, man's freedom is out of place because everything happens according to an inner necessity of a universal law. Even God is subject to this dialectical determination and becomes Mind or Spirit that develops in history.

Kierkegaard attacked Hegelianism vigorously and passionately. He reinstated the individual in his rightful place and restored to him his freedom. He underscored the fact that "Christianity begins by making every man an individual—an individual sinner."[92] Without this beginning

[88] Berdyaev, *Dream and Reality*, p. 102
[89] *Ibid.*, p. 103
[90] *Ibid.*, p. 96
[91] *Ibid.*, p. 95
[92] Sören Kierkegaard, *The Sickness unto Death*, trans. by Walter Lowrie (Princeton: Princeton University Press, 1941), p. 200

there can be no redemption. Kierkegaard stressed the
reality that the individual is he who has an infinite interest in himself and his destiny. As an individual, man feels
himself to be in a process of Becoming with a task before
him. Being a Christian is a matter of sustained effort. To
be a Christian is being in the state of constantly striving
to become one.

Kierkegaard's emphasis on the individual leads him to
conceive of existence chiefly in terms of what it means to
exist as an individual. As such, the individual is a center
of responsibility. His responsibility arises out of his freedom of choice. But the individual who is free and responsible finds himself also under the grip of forces beyond his control, arising from his own nature as well as
from the determinism of heredity and environment. "Man
is a synthesis of the infinite and the finite, of the temporal
and the eternal, of freedom and necessity."[93]

Man is determined and yet he is free. From one point of
view, he is eternal, and from another point of view, he is
temporal. He participates in the eternal and the temporal
at one and the same time. This paradoxical nature cannot
be resolved. But it is precisely in this paradoxical synthesis
that Kierkegaard discovers a condition of sheer possibility.
If man were absolutely conditioned by necessity or absolutely free, he would have no reason to despair, but also
he would not be a self. To be a person, a self, means to
have open possibilities: to negate or to affirm, to destroy
oneself or to edify oneself. This state of indeterminate
possibility, however, is a condition of anxiety. Each choice
and decision is a risk and a source of uncertainty and,
therefore, involves anxiety.

To exist, according to Kierkegaard, is to realize the indeterminate possibility. "Existence is the child that is born
of the infinite and the finite, the eternal and the tem-

[93] Sören Kierkegaard, *The Sickness unto Death*, p. 17

poral."[94] The existing individual, though he has the infinite within himself, is at the same time temporal and constantly in the process of becoming. As such, he is an existing subject.

Kierkegaard's dictum "Truth is subjectivity"[95] is not a description of any theory of knowledge but refers rather to the individual's mode of existence. Objective thinking directs the process of thinking away from the individual. It is preoccupied with results, and under its manipulation truth becomes an object. Objective thinking, in other words, makes the thinking subject incidental. It leads to abstract thought. Kierkegaard struggled against the tendency of his times to stress objectivity in thinking. Instead, he emphasized subjective thinking, in which the attention is turned to the subject. Subjective thinking regards the individual as an existing subject whose existence is a process of becoming. Existential thinking, in the Kierkegaardian sense, is subjective thinking. This subjectivity does not apply to scientific knowledge, but rather to ethico-religious truth. As such, subjective thinking is centered in inwardness.

Applied to Christianity, the difference between objectivity and subjectivity would be a "difference between knowing what Christianity is and being a Christian."[96] To approach Christianity objectively would be to acquire knowledge of, and study the facts about, Christianity. A Buddhist can do that and yet remain a Buddhist. To approach it subjectively would be to raise the question "How can I become a Christian?" and set out to become one. Subjectivity, therefore, implies continual striving without

[94] Kierkegaard, *Concluding Unscientific Postscript*, trans. by David F. Swenson; completed and edited by Walter Lowrie (Princeton: Princeton University Press and the American-Scandinavian Foundation, 1941), p. 85

[95] *Ibid.*, pp. 169–224

[96] *Ibid.*, p. 339

which human life disintegrates and man ceases to be a person. The passionate search for truth, says Kierkegaard, is better than objective certainty. He even goes further and insists that "an objective uncertainty held fast in an appropriation-process of the most passionate inwardness is the truth, the highest truth attainable for an existing individual."[97]

Certainty may be reached only by abstracting from existence in order to concentrate on the essences; in other words, by the individual becoming an abstract mind and ceasing to be a concrete person. This would mean leaving the self aside, by-passing it, and, with it, its passion, freedom and decision, which are inseparable from it. When that takes place, the individual ceases to be an individual and his personality is destroyed.

Needless to say, Kierkegaard reinforced Berdyaev in his opposition to Hegelianism. He showed him the dangerous cracks in the Hegelian philosophic structure, and, through his thesis, "Truth is subjectivity," provided him with an effective weapon with which to fight Hegelianism and promote individual freedom.

[97] Kierkegaard, *Concluding Unscientific Postscript*, p. 182

CHAPTER III

FREEDOM AND NECESSITY
(The Paradox)

1 A CONCEPTION OF MAN

Berdyaev's entire thinking is anthropocentric. The structure of his existential philosophy is erected on the foundation of his philosophical anthropology. His preoccupation with the problem of freedom arises out of his deep interest and personal involvement in man's predicament and destiny. Man is the chief object of his concern. At the heart of his thought lies a persistent attempt to understand what it means to be a person. Berdyaev's philosophy of freedom begins and ends with man.

> The essential and fundamental problem is the problem of man—of his knowledge, his freedom, his creativeness. Man is the key to the mystery of knowledge.[1]

Berdyaev's philosophical anthropology is thoroughly existential. It deals with man not as a concept but as a living person. The stress on man as an existing entity often leads Berdyaev to switch suddenly to the first person singular as in the following passage:

> Man cannot be left out of knowledge . . . I, a man, want to know reality, and the knowledge which may be attained in non-human realms is nothing to me. I, the knower, abide in reality . . . I know reality in and through myself, as man. Only an existent can know existence.[2]

[1] Berdyaev, *The Destiny of Man*, p. 11
[2] *Ibid.*, p. 11 f

What Berdyaev had come to know about existent man, chiefly through firsthand experience, constitutes both the sounding board and the springboard of his existential thinking. The very problem of freedom, the pivot of his philosophical thought, issues out of his conception of man, man's nature and man's destiny. For this reason, the first question that must be answered is: What is man according to Berdyaev?

For Berdyaev, man is a complex being with a dual nature. Man belongs at one and the same time to, and is the meeting place of, two worlds. He is both divine and human, heavenly and earthly, the child of God and the product of nature. Man is the point where two spheres intersect, the place at which they meet. He belongs to two different orders. "There is a spiritual man and there is a natural man, and yet the same individual is both spiritual and natural."[3] Man is conscious of the duality of his nature. He is aware of both his greatness and his worthlessness. "He knows himself as the image of God and as a drop in the ocean of the necessities of nature."[4]

The two natures in man are constantly in a state of war, both hot and cold, and man himself is the battleground. Now one of these natures, now the other seems to prevail.

Berdyaev does not claim originality in what he asserts about the duality of man's nature. "All deep thinkers have felt this,"[5] he says. He is especially cognizant, in this respect, of his affinity to Pascal, who "understood that the whole of Christianity is related to this duality of man's nature."[6] Berdyaev echoes the familiar words of Pascal:

[3] Berdyaev, *Freedom and the Spirit* (Original title: *Philosophy of the Free Spirit*, Paris, 1927), trans. by Oliver Fielding Clarke (New York: Charles Scribner's Sons, 1935), p. 27

[4] Berdyaev, *The Meaning of the Creative Act*, p. 60

[5] *Ibid.*

[6] *Ibid.*

> What a chimera is man! What a novelty! What a monster, what a contradiction, what a prodigy! Judge of all things, imbecile worm of the earth; depository of truth, a sink of uncertainty and error; the pride and refuse of the universe . . . know then, proud man, what a paradox you are to yourself![7]

when he writes:

> What a strange being—divided and of double meaning, having the form of a king and that of a slave, a being at once free and in chains, powerful and weak, uniting in one being glory and worthlessness, the eternal with the corruptible.[8]

The duality of man's nature is for Berdyaev the microscope through which he diagnoses man's predicament, and the telescope through which he attempts to discern man's destiny. Obviously, this dualism in man can be traced back to the Platonic doctrine of the two worlds, the world of phenomena and the world of ideas, which Berdyaev adopted in its Kantian revised version where the world of phenomena is equated with the world of necessity and the world of ideas or *things-in-themselves* is identified as the world of freedom.

In Berdyaev's view of man, we also find a Neo-Platonic flavor tempered with Boehme's mysticism.[9] Despite his dualism, man is nevertheless a microcosm. He is himself a small universe and not a fractional part of it.[10] Man and the cosmos measure their forces against each other, as equals.[11]

But man is not merely a microcosm. He is also a micro-

[7] Blaise Pascal, *Pensées—Provincial Letters* (New York: Modern Library, Inc., Random House, 1941), No. 434, p. 143

[8] Berdyaev, *The Meaning of the Creative Act*, p. 60

[9] Windelband, *A History of Philosophy*, p. 374. Cf. with Berdyaev, *The Meaning of the Creative Act*, p. 66

[10] Berdyaev, *The Meaning of History* (Berlin: 1923), trans. by George Reavey (London: Geoffrey Bles, 1936), p. 22

[11] Berdyaev, *The Meaning of the Creative Act*, p. 59

theos. This is so because "man is not only of this world but of another world; not only of necessity, but of freedom."[12] Belonging to two worlds, man is, therefore, "a self-contradictory and paradoxical being, combining opposite poles within himself."[13]

The thorny paradox of freedom and necessity grows out of Berdyaev's dualistic anthropology. Because of his dual nature, there are *two intentions* in man's "conscious mind, one which leads to the enslaving world of objects and to the realm of necessity, the other which is directed towards the truly existent world, the realm of freedom."[14]

Berdyaev's diagnosis of man's condition reveals that man has followed the first of the two intentions, namely, that which leads to the enslaving world of necessity. "The human spirit," he writes, "is in prison. Prison is what I call this world, the given world of necessity."[15]

This is the fundamental problem which confronts Berdyaev, demanding a positive solution. Man is a prisoner of necessity and he desperately needs to see the light and breathe the air of freedom. Berdyaev approached this dilemma with concern and enthusiasm. He made it his life-work to help bring about the liberation of man from the chains of necessity. And it is man as a living person, man as an existent being, who needs to be set free. In the task which Berdyaev sets for himself, he himself is existentially involved. "My sense of uprootedness and disestablishment in the world . . . is at the heart of my whole world outlook."[16]

What is the nature of the prison in which the human spirit is held captive, the prison which Berdyaev calls "this world, this given world of necessity"? The answer to this

[12] Berdyaev, *The Meaning of the Creative Act*, p. 61
[13] Berdyaev, *The Destiny of Man*, p. 46
[14] Berdyaev, *The Beginning and the End*, p. 59
[15] Berdyaev, *The Meaning of the Creative Act*, p. 11
[16] Berdyaev, *Dream and Reality*, p. 33

question may be discerned by discussing the four realms in which the paradoxical antithesis of freedom and necessity operates: nature, society, civilization, and history.

2 THE DETERMINISM OF NATURE

Necessity rules relentlessly in the realm of nature. Man is a natural being and is bound by many ties to the cosmos. He finds himself under the rule of natural necessity. His body is governed by natural processes, and is dependent on the soil, water, air, and sunshine for its very existence. Man is both nourished and destroyed by nature. He dies and his physical body is dissolved. Natural forces kill man, if not suddenly, then slowly. Nature is an order of determinism. Its laws demand obedience and submission. Man experiences natural necessity within himself and outside himself. He has to wrestle constantly with natural necessity and the power of his mind is his chief weapon.

Berdyaev distinguishes four periods in man's relationship to nature and the cosmos.[17] The first is that of man's submersion in cosmic life, when he was completely dependent on nature. In this primitive period, man's relation to nature was dominated by myth and magic. The second stage is characterized by man's partial liberation from the power of cosmic forces through the development of a primitive economy. Here also, he is freed from the superstitions concerning the demons in nature. In the third period, the mechanization of nature and its scientific and technical control take place. Industry is also developed and with it appears the complex problem of labor and management. Finally, there is the disruption of cosmic order in the discovery of the infinitely great and the infinitely small, the tremendous power of man over nature, and his enslavement by his own discoveries. Berdyaev foresaw a

[17] Berdyaev, *The Realm of Spirit and the Realm of Caesar*, p. 47 f

fifth period in the relationship between man and nature, when man's still greater control of nature's forces will be realized, and when man will also have control over his own technics and mechanization.

It is true, says Berdyaev, that the Renaissance witnessed a truce between man and nature. Nature was discovered, and man sought its many blessings. He became learner in its school, felt the enchantment of the outward appearance of nature, and was attracted by the joys of the natural life.[18] It is quite true that man gave up the struggle against nature which medieval man had waged. The Renaissance was concerned with a scientific as well as with an artistic discovery of nature. But that was not all. This early truce with nature was short-lived. In order to harness and utilize nature's forces, man was forced into war with nature itself which modern man has continued to carry on through his technology. Nature is still man's enemy. It still rules with its laws of necessity. "Nature, in its fallen state," says Berdyaev, "is wholly subject to causal determination and, as such, is the figure of necessity."[19]

It should be pointed out here that what Berdyaev means by nature is not limited to the physical universe. For him, nature has a much wider and deeper connotation. He explicitly states that by nature he does not mean "animals, plants, minerals nor stars, forests and seas."[20] Berdyaev does not use the term nature exclusively as an antithesis to civilization or even to the supernatural, nor as the cosmos or the creation, nor even as the world of matter and space. "To me," he explains, "nature is above all the contradiction of freedom; the order of nature is to be distinguished from the order of freedom."[21]

[18] Berdyaev, *The End of our Time*, p. 42 f
[19] Berdyaev, *Dream and Reality*, p. 106
[20] Berdyaev, *Slavery and Freedom*, p. 94
[21] *Ibid.*

If nature means the antithesis of freedom, then, by the same token, it is also the antithesis of personality and spirit. "Nature, in this sense, is the world of objectification, that is to say, of alienation, determinability, impersonality."[22] The slavery of man to nature is a slavery to that objectification, to that alienation, to that determinability. Often Berdyaev seems to use the term *nature* as equivalent to the *world* of the New Testament which is to be considered as hostile, as sinful. "This natural world is but the child of hatred and division, which in its turn engenders bondage and servitude."[23] "The natural world, 'this world,'" he also writes, "is the servitude, the enchainment of existence."[24]

Man's slavery to the world of things, to material necessity, is a crude form of slavery which can easily be detected. But there are other forms of man's slavery to nature, says Berdyaev, which are "more refined and less noticed."[25] He mentions, for instance, what he calls "the lure of the cosmos."[26] Berdyaev believes that there is in man a deep-seated desire to return to mother earth. This desire is often awakened and intensified by the overwhelming pressures of civilization and the heartaches and headaches of personal existence. Man seeks temporary relief by responding to "the lure of the cosmos." He turns to nature as a refuge from the demands of reason and the enslaving standards of civilization. Berdyaev does not mean here the occasional and recreational enjoyment of the beauty of nature. What he is referring to is the attempt to experience a fusion with cosmic life with the underlying assumption that nature itself is sacred. There are periods in history which are characterized by a return to nature as a guide

22 *Ibid.*
23 Berdyaev, *Freedom and the Spirit*, p. 17
24 Berdyaev, *Slavery and Freedom*, p. 95
25 *Ibid.*, p. 96
26 *Ibid.*

and as a lost paradise. This is what the romantics of all time try to do. The outstanding figure of the French Enlightenment, Jean Jacques Rousseau (1712–78) deified nature and thought that man came from it good and pure and that he had been alienated by civilization from his true nature. This "degeneration," according to Rousseau, could be stopped and eventually overcome and man would reach a state of perfection if he were given full freedom to develop according to his natural necessity.[27] The tendency to return to nature or to do things "according to nature" as well as the belief in the existence of a world-soul with which man may seek union may be observed in people seeking release from the demands and tensions of civilized life through exaltation of, and reliance on, such ties as those to race, soil, blood and sex.[28]

Berdyaev rejects a teleological, a mechanical, as well as a naturalistic interpretation of the world process on the ground that they all lead to an "ideal spiritual determinism."[29] This results in the loss of man's freedom and the enslavement of his personality. All attempts to realize freedom through fusion with cosmic life, such as those of all orgiastic cults, are founded on the belief in the possibility of "an ecstatic emergence beyond the boundaries of personal existence into the cosmic element," and on "the hope of entering into communion with this primary element."[30] Such attempts are based on illusions and deprive man of his personality and dignity. "Fusion with cosmic life does not emancipate personality, it brings about dissolution and annihilation."[31]

[27] Cf. Windelband, *A History of Philosophy*, p. 525 f
[28] Berdyaev, *Slavery and Freedom*, p. 97
[29] *Ibid.*
[30] *Ibid.*, p. 100
[31] *Ibid.*, p. 101

3 THE RULE OF SOCIETY

Man is not only a natural being. He is also a social being. He must, therefore, find self-realization in social life. He finds it necessary to live within a society. On society he must depend in his struggle for life against nature. Berdyaev thinks that man feels his relatedness to society even more keenly than his relation to nature.

The paradox of freedom and necessity operates in every social environment. Society both enriches and enslaves the life of man. It enriches when it seeks to establish unity among people and when the common struggle for survival and well-being is carried out by cooperative efforts.[32] Society is a blessing to man when it is conceived as a free union of men in the spirit of brotherhood. Society contributes to man's spiritual health and promotes his freedom when it takes the form of a religious togetherness, a *sobornost,* and when it is guided by the conviction that "the final goals of man's life are not social, but spiritual."[33]

Unfortunately, the influence of society's necessity upon man is much greater than that of its freedom. In his social relations, man often submits to the voice of necessity in society, which addresses him:

> You are my creation; everything that is best in you has been put there by me, and therefore you belong to me and you ought to give your whole self back to me.[34]

Even in its noble objective to induce and introduce cooperation and unity, society often uses coercive and unjust means. Having within himself not merely the need for bread, the symbol of the means of human existence, but

[32] Berdyaev, *The Beginning and the End,* p. 213

[33] Berdyaev, *The Realm of Spirit and the Realm of Caesar,* p. 62

[34] Berdyaev, *Slavery and Freedom,* p. 102

also the longing for world-wide unity, for fraternal association, man follows those who promise prosperity and security. The paradox of freedom and necessity persists in
the kind of world we have, with its evil, strife, and war.
"How can one combine the solution of the problem of
bread for everyone," Berdyaev asks, "a problem on which
human life depends, with the problem of freedom, on
which human dignity depends?"[35]

We understand the paradox of freedom and necessity
in society more clearly, and begin to see our way to its solution more distinctly, when we remember that there are
two ways of conceiving society and two paths that society
follows.[36] Society, according to Berdyaev, may be interpreted either as *nature* or as *spirit*. As nature, society is
ordered in accordance with the laws of nature, with the
rule of necessity as the guiding principle, and the struggle
for eventual predominance and mastery as the primary
motives, and force and compulsion as the executive means.
As spirit, society rests on the principle of personality with
a quest for freedom as its motivating goal and a passion for
love and mercy as its basic means. In actual experience,
society is both nature and spirit. Both principles, that of
necessity and that of freedom, are at work in it. But we
cannot deny the obvious fact that the natural in society
predominates over the spiritual, necessity over freedom,
coercive objectivity over free personality, the will to power
and mastery over love and mercy. The tragedy of man's
predicament is partly due to this fact.[37]

The conception of society as nature has been expressed
in what might be termed organic theories and organic in-
terpretations. The organic interpretation of society is in-

[35] Berdyaev, *The Realm of Spirit and the Realm of Caesar*,
p. 62. Cf. Berdyaev, *The Beginning and the End*, p. 216
[36] Berdyaev, *The Beginning and the End*, p. 217 ff
[37] *Ibid.*, p. 218 f

variably hierarchical. Society is thought of in terms of a higher personality that stands over and above the personality of the individual man, a larger personality that engulfs the individual one. Thus the primacy of society over the human personality is asserted, and man finds himself enslaved. The criterion of value is sought in the organism of society, which supposedly stands on a higher level than the human personality.

Berdyaev vehemently objects to the organic interpretation of society. He denies the existence of an organic principle for the organization of society. To claim the existence of such a principle is to give a false character of sacredness to things that are only relative. The organic in society is nothing but an illusion. As nature is partial, so is society partial. Not society, but man, is an organism. Society is an organization based on cooperation and coordination. As Berdyaev puts it, "man is the organism and society is his organ . . . The organic theory of society is a mere game in biological analogy."[38]

It is true, Berdyaev reminds us, that within society itself there are organic formations, such as the family, the tribe, as there are mechanical formations, like the club, the labor union. Both the organic and mechanical types of formations enslave man, the former more than the latter because it often claims sacredness.[39] Berdyaev mentions a third kind of human association within society which is spiritual in nature, namely, the church. "Only a spiritual community liberates man."[40] Unfortunately, because "some of the aspects of this spiritual life may be expressed in social forms . . . religion tends to become a social phenomenon and the Kingdom of God a social institution."[41]

[38] Berdyaev, *Slavery and Freedom*, p. 109 f

[39] *Ibid.*, p. 107 f

[40] *Ibid.*, p. 108

[41] Berdyaev, *Solitude and Society* (Paris: 1934), trans. by George Reavey (London: Geoffrey Bles, 1947), p. 75 f

The conflict of freedom and necessity in society arises out of the fact that man must live in a social environment, where law, order and authority are necessary, and yet his personality "can never be a part of society, because it can never be a part of anything."[42] On the one hand, "society is an infinitely more powerful thing than the personality"; and on the other hand, "personality affirms its supreme value even in the sphere of social life."[43] In this paradoxical situation man finds himself and it causes him much pain and suffering.

4 THE DOMINATION OF CIVILIZATION

The battle between freedom and necessity is also fought in the world made by man, the very civilization he creates for the purpose of liberating himself from natural necessity. In this man-made domain, the paradox of freedom and necessity appears in a more frightening form.

What Berdyaev means by civilization and the distinction he makes between it and culture must be borne in mind. This is important because civilization is commonly taken to mean culture as well. He stresses the fact, first of all, that "in a certain sense civilization is older and more primitive than culture, culture takes shape later. The invention of technical equipment, even of the most elementary tools by primitive man is civilization, just as civilization is the whole socializing process."[44] According to Berdyaev, civilization is concerned with man's physical survival, while culture aims at his intellectual and spiritual development. Civilization is closer to nature and necessity, and culture is nearer to spirit and freedom.

By civilization must be meant a process which is more social

[42] Berdyaev, *Solitude and Society*, p. 137
[43] *Ibid.*, p. 136
[44] Berdyaev, *Slavery and Freedom*, p. 122

and collective, by culture, a process which is more individual
and which goes deeper.[45]

> Civilization indicates a higher degree of objectification and
> socialization, whereas culture is more closely linked with per-
> sonality and spirit. Culture indicates . . . the victory of form
> over matter.[46]

Man creates a civilization in order to set himself free
from the forces of nature and their enslaving necessity.
Civilization was initiated by the invention of primitive
tools which man continued to improve and increase. The
conquest of nature stimulated the cooperative effort of
men and called for organization of their lives.

The most revolutionary event in the history of civilization is the emergence of a technological knowledge with
the triumphant advance of the machine. The whole structure of civilization was remolded by the technological progress. Through his technical skill, man has been able to
harness the forces of nature and subordinate them to his
own purposes. The splitting of the atom and man's initial
thrust into outer space are only the beginning of a cosmic
revolution which is the fruit of modern civilization.

It would seem rather banal and quite unnecessary, says
Berdyaev, to enumerate the blessings of civilization in all
its various provinces. He has no quarrel with the positive
aspect of our technological civilization. But he does stub-
bornly take issue with its negative results.

> Civilization promises to emancipate man and there can be
> no dispute that it provides the equipment for emancipation;
> but it is also the objectification of human existence and, there-
> fore, it brings enslavement with it. Man is made the slave of
> civilization.[47]

[45] *Ibid.*
[46] *Ibid.*
[47] *Ibid.*, p. 118

Civilization is the theme of man's struggle with, and triumph over, the tyranny of natural necessity. But periodically, as it has already been noted, man has returned to nature seeking liberation from civilization which, after freeing him from the chains of nature, shackled him with glittering fetters of its own. Civilization arose as a means, but soon it was turned into an end. It has become a tremendous power which controls man. Man himself has become a means for the realization of the technical and industrial process of civilization. The continuous growth of the multiplicity of things in daily life crushes man. Who has not felt the powerful grip of things!

> Technical progress testifies not only to man's strength and power over nature; it not only liberates man but also weakens and enslaves him; it mechanizes human life and gives man the image and semblance of a machine.[48]

Like most existentialists, Berdyaev deplores the mechanization of life and the enslavement of man by the very machine he created. It is the machine that replaced man and thus plagued him with unemployment. "The machine has a crushing effect on the human soul, it damages emotional life first of all, thus shattering the integrity of the human personality."[49]

Machinery has destroyed the unity of human life. Modern technology has placed in man's hands a fearful instrument of destruction and has, therefore, surrounded his existence with an atmosphere of fear and anxiety. Our overorganized civilization demands of man an evergrowing activity, but by this demand it enslaves him and turns him into a mechanism. This is partly due to the change in man's relation to time.

[48] Berdyaev, *The Destiny of Man*, p. 225 f
[49] Berdyaev, *The Fate of Man in the Modern World* (Paris: 1934), trans. by Donald Lowrie (New York: Morehouse Publishing Co., 1935), p. 73

Through the conquest of time by the machine, time itself has undergone an acceleration to which the rhythm of human life must respond. Our civilization is entirely oriented toward the future. Each moment is but a means to the succeeding moment. Our world is a world of mathematical time measured by the calendar and the clock.

Swept away by the torrent of time, man does not have adequate time to assert himself as the free creator of his future. Applied to economic life, the new conception of time gives rise to a utilitarian estimate of man. Man's value is dependent upon his productivity within a given time. This leads slowly but surely to the destruction of man's personality.[50]

One of the most unfortunate results of modern technological and industrial civilization is the appearance of vast impersonal masses of people. It is the negative effects of civilization that produce the mass man, to whatever class he may belong. The main characteristics that distinguish the man who belongs to the masses are

> a lack of expressed personality, the absence of personal originality, a disposition to swim with the current of the quantitative force of any given moment, an extraordinary susceptibility to mental contagion, imitativeness, repeatability.[51]

The mass man, in Berdyaev's view, appropriates the technical side of civilization, but is able to assimilate spiritual culture only with difficulty and reluctance, if at all. "The masses in the present transitional period," says Berdyaev, "are devoid of all spiritual culture."[52] This is another way of saying that the masses of today are chained by modern technology and are enslaved by its necessity. They have surrendered their freedom as a price for ma-

[50] Berdyaev, *The Realm of Spirit and the Realm of Caesar*, p. 51
[51] Berdyaev, *Slavery and Freedom*, p. 121
[52] *Ibid.*, p. 121 f

terialistic satisfactions; and without freedom there can be
no spiritual culture.

What adds intensity to the seriousness of man's predicament is the fact that culture itself, which is meant to be
an agent of freedom, is gravely endangered by a "process
of democratization and leveling-down, by the domination
of the mass."[53] The crisis of culture in our times lies in
the stress on quantity at the expense of quality. It is increasingly demanded of culture that it be watered down to
correspond to the needs and desires of the masses.[54] "The
mass determines what shall be the accepted culture, art,
literature, philosophy, science, even religion."[55] Culture
is undergoing such drastic changes, says Berdyaev, that it
needs a new name. Besides this process of "democratization" of culture and its resultant mass production, there is
also the danger arising out of the tendency in man to idol-
ize his own cultural creations and to become a slave to his
own cultural values.[56] And whenever and wherever that
happens, man finds himself behind the bars of necessity.
Thus in the sphere of civilization and despite the cultural
creativeness of man, the paradox of freedom and necessity
remains unresolved. Its tension continues to plague man.

5   THE GRIP OF HISTORY

A head-on collision between freedom and necessity takes
place in history. In the realm of the historical, Berdyaev
discerns the most paradoxical form of man's predicament.
This is so because "without freedom there is no history but
only the realm of nature. Yet at the same time history sup-
presses the freedom of man; it subordinates him to its own
necessities."[57]

[53] Berdyaev, *The Fate of Man in the Modern World*, p. 100
[54] *Ibid.*, p. 101
[55] *Ibid.*, p. 101 f
[56] Berdyaev, *Slavery and Freedom*, p. 129
[57] Berdyaev, *The Divine and the Human* (original title: *The*

We shall address ourselves first to the first part of this paradox, namely, that "history presupposes freedom,"[58] which receives in Berdyaev's books generous reiteration but inadequate interpretation. Perhaps the key that might unlock Berdyaev's meaning is found in his statement: "History postulates the freedom of man. The determinism of nature cannot be transferred to history."[59] Nature does not presuppose freedom, as far as man is concerned, because it existed before man and man is not the maker of nature. Man's relation to history with respect to freedom, however, is different. History presupposes man's existence and, therefore, his freedom. It is the result of the creative or destructive activity of his freedom. It is true that man is a historical being, born into a historical epoch and must realize himself in history, but it is also true that "it is man that makes history . . . and that it is to be supposed that he makes history for his own sake."[60] "History is also my history. I have indeed had a share in its happening."[61] Again, Berdyaev states, "I accept history not because I am part of history but because history is part of me. That means that I accept it not as an obedient slave but as a free man."[62]

It is one of the fundamental tenets of Berdyaev's philosophy of history that the freedom of the spirit belongs to him who does not conceive of history "as an exterior imposition" but rather "as an interior event of spiritual significance, that is, the expression of freedom."[63] "Only

---

Existential Dialectic of the Divine and the Human, Paris: 1947), trans. by R. M. French (London: Geoffrey Bles, 1949), p. 178

[58] Berdyaev, *The Beginning and the End*, p. 209

[59] *Ibid.*

[60] Berdyaev, *Truth and Revelation*, trans. by R. M. French (New York: Harper & Brothers, 1953), p. 79

[61] *Ibid.*, p. 81

[62] *Ibid.*, p. 82

[63] Berdyaev, *The Meaning of History*, p. 38

in such a free and emancipating view," Berdyaev goes on to say, "can history be understood as the expression of man's inner freedom."[64]

It might add more light to what Berdyaev means by the words "history postulates the freedom of man" to mention also that, in his opinion, there are two major elements in history: the conservative and the creative.[65] The first refers to the tie with the past through its heritage, the second is identified with man's dynamic and creative drive toward self-fulfillment. No historical process is possible without the union of these two elements. "The absence of either of these two elements invalidates the postulate of history."[66] Man's debt to the past must be translated into a duty toward the future, a duty which expresses itself in free creative activity that becomes a part of history.

As a historical being, man must live in time which, according to Berdyaev, has three dimensions: cosmic time, historical time, and existential time.[67] Cosmic time may be symbolized by the circle. It is the time which is related to the movement of the earth, and is divided into years, months, days, hours, minutes, and seconds. This is, so to speak, nature's time, and as a natural being, man lives in cosmic time.

Man lives also in historical time. History is also subject to cosmic time. It is measured by centuries and years, but it has its own historical time which is the result of the movement and change of man and society. Historical time may be symbolized by the straight line reaching into the past and into the future. Its direction is toward the future. It is true that in historical time there is also return and repetition as is the case in cosmic time. There are strong

---

[64] Berdyaev, *The Meaning of History*, p. 38
[65] *Ibid.*, p. 39
[66] *Ibid.*
[67] Berdyaev, *Slavery and Freedom*, p. 257

resemblances between certain periods of history. But, nevertheless, the novel element dominates. Every event in historical time is in a sense unique; and every year, decade, and century introduces a new life and new happenings. Historical time has a closer connection with human activity than cosmic time.

There is also existential time. This should not be thought of in complete isolation from cosmic and historical time. The symbol of existential time is the point. This kind of time is not computed mathematically. It is not summed up nor divided into parts. Existential time, writes Berdyaev, is "the irruption of eternity into time . . . It is the time of the world of subjectivity . . . A moment of existential time is an emergence into eternity."[68] Man's creative activity, for instance, is performed in existential time and is merely projected into historical time. It is this projection, this *objectification*, which results in the tragic conflict between man and history.

History, whether it studies the universe or man, is an interpretation of what has been but is no more. As such, it is primarily an objective process insofar as it investigates the past as an object. It is, consequently, relegated, like nature, to the objective world. By virtue of its objective nature, history is indifferent to man and his personality. This indifference is potentially capable of turning man into a tool for the actualization of history. When this happens, he becomes a statistical unit in historical events and records.[69]

Never before has man been more at the mercy of the processes at work in history than he is in our times. No person escapes the effect of the historical event of today. The fatality of history tends to reduce all men to a common level. History does not give man any promises or

[68] *Ibid.*, p. 260
[69] Berdyaev, *The Fate of Man in the Modern World*, p. 4 f

guarantees. "History needed man as its material, but has not recognized him as her purpose."[70]

What adds to man's misery in and through history is the fact that often he himself deifies history and regards its processes as sacred. Not infrequently, he is willing to bow his head and knee to historical necessity, which thus itself becomes a criterion of values; and obedience to this necessity is regarded as the only freedom he possesses.[71]

Berdyaev allocates a substantial amount of blame for man's predicament in history to Hegel who considered all history as sacred. Hegel also thought of history as the victorious march of the Spirit toward freedom. The concept of freedom occupies a prominent place in Hegel's philosophy, but it is a freedom within the frame of necessity. For Hegel, necessity, *Notwendigkeit*, has two different meanings: the one is identical with external motivation, and the other is equated with internal self-regulation. The latter kind of necessity Hegel calls freedom.

> Necessity . . . in the ordinary acceptation of the term in popular philosophy means determination from without only— as in finite mechanics, where a body moves only when it is struck by another body, and moves in the direction communicated to it by the impact. This, however, is a merely external necessity, not the real inward necessity which is identical with freedom.[72]

Like Kierkegaard and Dostoyevsky before him, Berdyaev protested against Hegel's idea of a universal Spirit revealing itself in history. Hegel wanted to sacrifice man and his human existence on the altar of his philosophy of history. To history, Hegel subordinated not only man

[70] Berdyaev, *The Fate of Man in the Modern World*, p. 16
[71] Berdyaev, *Slavery and Freedom*, p. 256
[72] G.W.F. Hegel, *The Logic of Hegel*, trans. by W. Wallace (London: Oxford University Press, 1950), Second Edition, Sect. 35, p. 71

but also God, who, in his view, is the creation of history itself. The implications of Hegelian philosophy would be the unconditional surrender and obedience to the conquerors in history and the acknowledgment of them as instruments for the realization of the Spirit which, according to Hegel, is freedom. Hegel's freedom is the freedom of the universal and not of the individual. Hegel's philosophy of freedom actually denied freedom by acknowledging it as the product of necessity and, at times, necessity itself.[73]

There is something in man, says Berdyaev, which makes him rebel against being converted into a means employed by a pitiless and inhuman historical process.

> On the one hand I accept history as my path, the path of man, and on the other hand I indignantly tear the mask from it and rebel against it . . . History has set its ineffaceable stamp upon me. Yet at the same time I am a free spirit, a person who bears the image and likeness of God, not only the image of the world . . . One must preserve one's freedom in the realm of necessity.[74]

History is then an arena of the unresolved conflict between freedom and necessity. Man himself makes history, but history takes no account of him and often uses him as fuel in the struggle between classes, nations, faiths, and ideas. The clash between history and human personality is never resolved within historical time because man cannot cease to be a historical being. Men try to escape this paradox through historical pessimism. They surrender to irrational fate, but find that the chains of their slavery have become heavier. More often, the escape takes the direction of historical optimism. Men are lured by the mirage of progress and are moved by dreams of Utopia

[73] Cf. G.W.F. Hegel, *Lectures on the Philosophy of History*, trans. by J. Sibree (New York: 1944).
[74] Berdyaev, *Truth and Revelation*, p. 80 f

4

but sooner or later find themselves stranded in the scourging desert of disillusionment. For Berdyaev, the solution of the paradox of freedom and necessity does not lie within history. He cannot rest his faith on the uncertain facts of historical time. "Many a soul has lost its faith on the shifting sand of these historical facts."[75]

[75] Berdyaev, *Dream and Reality*, p. 299

CHAPTER IV

FREEDOM AND PERSONALITY

(The Implications)

1 THE DYNAMICS OF PERSONALITY

Berdyaev's anthropology is strictly personalistic, and so is his philosophy, which he sometimes describes as a philosophy of personalism. His *summum bonum* is the human personality, its self-realization, its development and progress in the attainment of truth and beauty.[1] Everything is seen from the viewpoint of personality. Everything is evaluated by the nature of its effect on the human personality.

But man's personality, Berdyaev immediately insists, can exist only in the spiritual climate of freedom. Its self-fulfillment is realized in and through freedom. Freedom is, as it were, the diet on which personality feeds and the oxygen it breathes. In the words of Berdyaev,

> The personality is not only related to freedom but cannot exist without it. To realize the personality is therefore to achieve inner freedom, to liberate man from all external determination.[2]

This vital relationship between freedom and personality makes a study of Berdyaev's concept of personality a prerequisite to the understanding of his philosophy of freedom.

[1] Berdyaev, *Solitude and Society*, p. 149
[2] *Ibid.*

What is personality according to Berdyaev? Personality
is not a biological or a psychological, but rather an ethical
entity.[3] It is not a natural but a spiritual category. By
nature, man is an individual; by spirit, he is a personality.
We may say of a man that he lacks personality, but we
cannot deny him individuality. Personality is not the soul
as distinct from the body. Berdyaev rejects the dualism of
soul and body and advocates a "vital unity of soul and
body in man."[4] Soul and body mutually permeate each
other. The dualism for him exists not between soul and
body, but between spirit and nature, between freedom and
necessity; and personality is a certain condition which
exists between the opposites of this dualism, namely,
"the victory of the spirit over nature, of freedom over necessity."[5]

Personality, therefore, belongs to an entirely different
order than that of soul and body. It is "not born of a
father and mother . . . Personality in man is not determined by heredity, biological and social."[6] Personality is
rather and "above all an 'axiological' category: it is the
manifestation of an existential purpose."[7] It should not
be conceived in substantial terms but should be understood as "the absolute existential centre"[8] which determines itself from within.

The definition of personality by Max Scheler as the
union of our acts and their potentialities seems to appeal
to Berdyaev.[9] Yet, personality is more than that. Berdyaev
writes:

[3] Berdyaev, *Slavery and Freedom*, p. 25
[4] *Ibid.*, p. 31
[5] *Ibid.*
[6] *Ibid.*, p. 36
[7] Berdyaev, *Solitude and Society*, p. 122
[8] Berdyaev, *Slavery and Freedom*, p. 26
[9] Berdyaev, *Solitude and Society*, p. 122; cf. Max Scheler, *Der
Formalismus in der Ethik und die materiale Wertethik* (1916)

When confronted with the personality, I am in the presence of a Thou. It is not an object, a thing, or a substance; nor is it an objectified form of psychic life—the object of psychology.[10]

Here Berdyaev echoes Martin Buber's I-Thou relationship. But in his contrast of personality with *thing*, he reflects the influence of William Stern, a contemporary psychologist and philosopher, whose personalist philosophy rests on the assumption that the person is a psychological unity, characterized by purposiveness and individuality.[11] Berdyaev refers to Stern's contribution and finds in this thinker's antithetical terms *Person und Sache*, person and thing, a distinction which replaces the traditional one between spirit and matter.[12]

Stern defines personality as that existential entity which, despite its multiplicity, is capable of constituting "a unity possessed of originality and value," and of forming, despite the multiplicity of its functions, "a unity endowed with independence and finality."[13]

The essential quality of personality is its *unitas multiplex*. As such, it is an integral whole, not a sum of parts. It is an end in itself, unlike the thing, which is a means to an end. A fundamental characteristic of the personality is its capacity to be a free agent.

Berdyaev goes along with Stern up to this point. He disagrees with him as soon as Stern begins to elaborate a whole hierarchy of overlapping personalities into which he admits collectives such as the nation. For Berdyaev, this

[10] Berdyaev, *Solitude and Society*, p. 123
[11] William Stern, "Die Psychologie und der Personalismus." *Zeitschrift für Psychologie* 78, 1917; cf. Dagobert D. Runes, *The Dictionary of Philosophy* (New York: Philosophical Library, 1942), p. 301
[12] Berdyaev, *Solitude and Society*, p. 124
[13] *Ibid.*; cf. William Stern, *Person und Sache: System des kritischen Personalismus* (Leipzig), 3 volumes, 1923–24.

elaboration is anathema and unforgivable. In his view, it makes Stern's supposedly personalistic philosophy too rationalistic and, therefore, it "cannot claim to be strictly existential."[14]

Berdyaev goes beyond Stern to state "another most important property" in which the personality radically differs from the thing, namely, "being able to experience joy and suffering" and being endowed with "the sense of a unique and indivisible destiny."[15] "Personality is my whole thinking, my whole willing, my whole feeling, my whole creative activity."[16]

In an effort to clarify his concept of personality, Berdyaev calls attention to the fact that the Latin word *persona* signifies a *mask* and has theatrical associations. "The personality is essentially a mask. Man employs it not only to disclose himself to the world, but also to defend himself from its importunity."[17] This should be understood in a positive way. Personality as a mask implies "a task to be achieved."[18] Its pulse is the creative act. Its aim is the triumph over all sorts of determinations.

> Personality is activity, opposition, victory over the dragging burden of the world, the triumph of freedom over the world's slavery. The fear of exertion is harmful to the realization of personality. Personality is effort and conflict, the conquest of self and of the world, victory over slavery, it is emancipation.[19]

As a task to be accomplished, as a creative activity, personality is constantly in a process of change. It requires time for the actualization of its potentialities. But with the change there is also the element of immutability in

[14] Berdyaev, *Solitude and Society*, p. 124
[15] *Ibid.*
[16] Berdyaev, *Slavery and Freedom*, p. 25
[17] Berdyaev, *Solitude and Society*, p. 125
[18] Berdyaev, *Dream and Reality*, p. 55
[19] Berdyaev, *Slavery and Freedom*, p. 24

personality. This accounts for its paradoxical nature. This paradox in personality expresses itself also in the fact that, on the one hand, personality is potentially universal, and, on the other hand, it is a distinct, unrepeatable, irreplaceable being, unique in every respect. "The secret of the existence of personality lies in its absolute irreplaceability, its happening but once, its uniqueness, its incomparableness."[20]

Personality is a religious and spiritual category. Seen in the Christian context, it is "the image and likeness of God in man and this is why it rises above the natural life."[21] As such, personality is not a part of something but a unity possessing absolute worth. Its value is intrinsic and cannot be reduced to a common denominator. Man's worth is the personality within him.

Personality is the reflection of the divine image and likeness, and, consequently, it is the true path leading to God. Man is given the power to become a personality. He must be afforded every opportunity of achieving this. But the process requires great efforts on his part. The struggle to become a personality, integrated and consolidated, is a painful process. This is so because strong resistance is constantly encountered and a conflict with the enslaving power of the world ensues. But it is precisely in the heat of the struggle that the fruits of freedom ripen. The quest for freedom, and personality is freedom, inevitably involves suffering and a "capacity to bear pain."[22]

The path of the realization of personality is paved with love and sacrifice. Love and sacrifice constitute the relationship of one personality to another. They are the means by which the personality is freed from the prison of self. They are the channels by which the personality identifies

[20] *Ibid.*, p. 23
[21] Berdyaev, *Dream and Reality*, p. 55
[22] Berdyaev, *Slavery and Freedom*, p. 28

itself with another personality. Sacrifice is the medium
through which the uniqueness is respected. This means
that the personality grows and expands only in relation to
another personality. The recognition of each personality's
uniqueness, that it constitutes a Thou, is essential to our
understanding of the mystery of love.

> To be in love with another's personality is to perceive the
> identity and unity underlying its perpetual change and division;
> it is to perceive its nobility even in the midst of utter deg-
> radation.[23]

From the point of view of ethics, Berdyaev reminds us,
personality is linked with character. A strong personality
implies a strong character; and a strong character signifies
the victory of the spiritual principle in man. True morality
begins with power over oneself and ends with triumph
over slavery to oneself. This must precede any victory over
the enslavement to this world. "Character is conquest and
attainment; it presupposes freedom."[24] A good character
is an indication that a person has established distinctions,
is not indifferent, but has made his choice. Such a person
is neither blind nor enslaved to the status quo or to conventions. The personality of such a man is free.

Despite his stress on the close relationship between
personality and morality, Berdyaev registers his disagree-
ment with Kant, who passes over from the intellectual to
the ethical conception of personality. According to Kant,
"morality alone makes the person a person, the self a
self."[25] In the Kantian sense, and as Professor Kroner
put it,

> That which is called "character" in the strictly moral sense

[23] Berdyaev, *Solitude and Society*, p. 147

[24] Berdyaev, *Slavery and Freedom*, p. 47

[25] Richard Kroner, *Speculation and Revelation in Modern Philosophy* (Philadelphia: The Westminster Press, 1961), p. 221

is not identical with the "nature" of an individual, but it depends upon the free decisions and actions of the person. I am responsible for my character; I myself am its author.[26]

Because of this fact, personality is not just a phenomenon among other phenomena. Personality is an end in itself, not a means to an end; it exists through itself. "Nevertheless," concludes Berdyaev, "Kant's doctrine of personality is not true personalism because the value of personality is defined by its moral and rational nature, which comes into the category of the universal."[27]

According to Berdyaev, the existence of the human personality with its loves and fears, with its hopes and anxieties, with its unique and unrepeatable destiny, is a paradox in the world of nature and within the confines of society, civilization, and history. Personality is unceasingly faced with an environment which is alien to it. The human personality with its aspirations, and the conditions of existence in this world are contradictory to each other and cannot but clash. In the process of its self-realization, personality must constantly struggle against the forces of estrangement and exteriorization, against what Berdyaev calls the principle of objectification which enslaves man by its chains of necessity and threatens his freedom with the fetters of causality. What Berdyaev means by this term is the next question for discussion.

2   THE PRINCIPLE OF OBJECTIFICATION

Objectification is a fundamental concept in Berdyaev's philosophy. It is a principle that operates in the " 'objective world', i.e. the world of our natural and historical environment."[28] Objectification is the process by which a subject is converted into an object. The most common and easily

[26] *Ibid.*, p. 222
[27] Berdyaev, *Slavery and Freedom*, p. 34
[28] Berdyaev, *Dream and Reality*, p. 286

4*

recognizable objectification takes place whenever a person, a spiritual entity, is treated as a thing, as an object, as a commodity. Whenever a human being is used as a means rather than as an end, objectification occurs. Everything, including God, may be, and generally is, liable to be objectified.

The principle of objectification occupies a vital role in Berdyaev's dualistic world. It is a one-way bridge leading from the higher and real world, the realm of freedom, to the lower and unreal world, the realm of necessity. "Objectification is a symbolical description of the fallen state of a world in which man finds himself subservient to necessity and disunion."[29]

The bridge of objectification on which spiritual realities, *things-in-themselves*, slide down into the ocean of necessity, into the world of phenomena, is itself located in man's mind and is constructed on wrong social and spiritual attitudes of hatred and injustice, of disdain and prejudice. Operating through abstraction, objectification invariably leads to the burning fires of dehumanization, depersonalization and degradation. It prevails in most social relations, which are characterized by superficial and impersonal contacts and in which the person's spiritual status is not recognized. Berdyaev often alludes to the world in which such conditions exist as the "fallen world." It is the world in which society is no longer knit by spiritual ties. It is a world in which the I-Thou relationship has been replaced by the I-It relationship.

People practice the principle of objectification more than they realize. Often, objectification becomes their second nature and they begin to think of it as quite normal. When that happens, they become spiritually bankrupt and self-alienated. Objectification is a disease which drains off man's spiritual qualities. Man ceases to be self-directed

[29] Berdyaev, *Dream and Reality*, p. 288

and becomes other-directed. Life degenerates into mere accommodation to what is common and average. It becomes geared to external norms and standards. Inner motivation disappears and its function is taken over by social customs and conventions, by the rule of expediency and convenience. Man is no longer a creator but an imitator. He loses his freedom and becomes a slave. To use Berdyaev's own words, "in the process of objectification the subjective spirit loses its identity."[30]

Objectification is the ejection of man into the external, it is an exteriorization of him, it is the subjection of him to the conditions of space, time, causality and rationalization.[31]

To sum up, Berdyaev considers the following to be the main characteristics of objectification:

1 The estrangement of the object from the subject.
2 The absorption of the unrepeatably individual and personal in what is common and impersonally universal.
3 The rule of necessity, of determination from without, the crushing of freedom and the concealment of it.
4 Adjustment to the grandiose mien of the world of history, to the average man, and the socialization of man and his opinions, which destroys distinctive character.[32]

The process of objectification operates not only in society and people but also in nature and things. Berdyaev makes a distinction between the creative activity and the created product. While the former is a part of the noumenal world and is free from objectification, the latter is a part of the phenomenal world and is affected by objectification.[33] The symphony which a composer creates, for

[30] Berdyaev, *Spirit and Reality* (Paris: 1937), trans. by George Reavey (London: Geoffrey Bles, 1939), p. 49
[31] Berdyaev, *The Beginning and the End*, p. 60
[32] *Ibid.*, p. 62
[33] *Ibid.*, p. 181

instance, is a part of the objectified world, but the creative
activity by which the symphony was composed is part of
the world of spirit and freedom. It is in this sense that
Berdyaev also equates objectification with materialization
of spiritual entities. Man has a tendency to worship the
product of his creation. This results in his enslavement to
and by the things he produces. This explains the fact, Berdyaev points out, that property can be on the one hand a
source of freedom and independence, and, on the other
hand, an agent of man's slavery. Exploitation and abuse of
natural resources lead to their objectification. Living exclusively by and for the power of money and the things
that power can buy objectifies man's spirit. As a result,
man is no longer defined by what he is but by what he
has.

Berdyaev makes a deductive statement that "the world
of appearance is the outcome of objectification."[34] Objects are all created by subjects. The "fallen world," in
other words, is man-made. It must be noted that the
attempt to understand "the world as a product of spirit,
to comprehend even the corporeal world with all its phenomena as essentially intellectual or spiritual in its origin
and content," as Windelband has shown, is nothing
new.[35] It was the "final result of ancient philosophy" to
conceive the world in this manner.[36]

In his theory of objectification, Berdyaev has a close
affinity to the German idealists who thought that the
world is *my idea* or, as Schopenhauer often called it, a
"phenomenon of the brain."[37] Schopenhauer, who identified Kant's *thing-in-itself* with the Will, but who denied
any causal relation between the *thing-in-itself* and the

[34] Berdyaev, *The Beginning and the End*, p. 53
[35] Windelband, *A History of Philosophy*, p. 235
[36] *Ibid.*
[37] *Ibid.*, p. 588

world of phenomena, nevertheless regarded phenomenal nature as objectification, that is, "as the perceptional and conceptional mode of representation of the will or the immediately real."[38] It may be noted in passing, as Matthew Spinka has pointed out, that Karl Marx, during his early period, formulated his basic concept of "social injustice in terms of *Verdinglichung* (objectification), i.e., as the treatment of the proletarians as things, as a commodity."[39]

But Berdyaev differs from the German idealists in his assertion that the agent of objectification is not the suprapersonal Spirit or Absolute Idea but the human spirit itself. The objectification of the world through human manipulation turns the freedom of noumena into the necessity of phenomena.[40] In other words, it results in the loss of freedom.

For Berdyaev, the objectified world is not the true and real world. It is only a symbol of the real world of the spirit. But the awareness that anything in this world is merely a symbol of another world has a positive function. It helps in liberating man from a slavish dependence on this world. This theory will be developed in detail later.

In the area of knowledge, objectification implies that the knower and the known are mutually alien. Applied to persons, it means *knowing about* them rather than *knowing them*. In this respect there is an essential difference between natural sciences and the humanities. In natural sciences, objectification does not destroy the object of knowledge, since nature itself is the result of objectification. In the humanities and in the realm of the spirit, objectification leads to the destruction of the reality which we seek to know.

[38] *Ibid.*, p. 589

[39] Matthew Spinka, *Nicolas Berdyaev: Captive of Freedom* (Philadelphia: The Westminster Press, 1950), p. 109

[40] Berdyaev, *The Beginning and the End*, p. 56

Through the process of objectification, the true Church, as a non-authoritarian spiritual entity, as a spiritual union and communion in love and freedom, is transformed into an authoritarian social institution with conflicts within and without and with worldly ambitions. No wonder that the visible and historic church often alienates people from God. Fortunately, the earnest and faithful Christian can always transcend the objectified church and can be a part of the life of the true Church, the *sobornost*, which is sustained by the indwelling Spirit of the risen Lord.

> The historical Church reminds one of other historical bodies, is very similar to the State, to the kingdom of Caesar . . . It also is subject to the power of necessity. But the Church is also meta-historical; another world beyond this world is disclosed in it. It is a spiritual society; the realm of freedom is in it.[41]

3 DEPERSONALIZATION AND DEHUMANIZATION

The process of objectification is the chief enemy of man, his personality and his freedom. It lies at the heart of the dehumanization of modern man and the depersonalization of his personality. The principle of objectification, Berdyaev thinks, accounts for the crumbling of civilizations. This principle, by which subjects are turned into objects, operates in man's own mind.

Berdyaev underscores, first of all, the overturning of the hierarchy of values as the most dangerous and most consequential product of objectification. Those values which rank high, such as truth, beauty, goodness, and freedom are brought lower, and those which are at the bottom of the scale, such as expediency, usefulness, exploitation, and violence are elevated to the top. Putting the matter in terms of means and ends, the means in man's life, such as economics and politics, become ends in themselves. "The

[41] Berdyaev, *The Divine and the Human*, p. 179 f

means take central place, and the ends are either forgotten, or become purely rhetorical."[42]

Berdyaev convincingly shows how this reversal of values is characteristic of our times. The real aims of human life have been displaced. Man's life is filled with an abundance of the means of living but has been alarmingly emptied of the ends which make life worth living. Man has forgotten the *why* of living and is preoccupied with the *know-how*. He is too busy to think about the meaning and the purpose of life. For him the means have an immediate reality but the aims, which he has deposited in the attic of his mind, have no reality at all.

Behind this displacement of values is a pragmatic outlook, itself the outcome of objectification, which makes the usefulness of a thing or a being determine its place on the scale of values. In determining the value of entities, their qualities and quantities, the element of truth is totally ignored. "One of the worst evils," warns Berdyaev, "is a utilitarian attitude toward truth."[43] Man has the devious illusion that the truth is his servant. There is no awareness that he has been called to serve the truth.

Berdyaev notes that part of the same confusion in values is the widespread prevalence of the principle that the end justifies the means. Evil means are being used to achieve good ends, means which contradict the very ends sought. Christianity is no exception. Its history is checkered with dark means and bright ends. In Europe, the attempt was made to spread the Christian message of love and forgiveness by blood and violence. The phantom of the professional Christian inquisitor darkens many decades of church history. Evil means have weakened rather than strengthened the church. The noble ends of the French Revolution were lost in the terror and violence of the guillotine.

[42] Berdyaev, *The Realm of Spirit and the Realm of Caesar*, p. 88

[43] *Ibid.*, p. 91

Berdyaev cites with bitter criticism "the dehumanization and bestialization" of our times, the "barbaric forms of cruelty" of our modern society, and, with sarcasm, the "bestialism" which "is something quite different from the old, natural, healthy barbarism; it is barbarism within a refined civilization." "Here," he continues, "the atavistic, barbaric instincts are filtered through the prism of civilization, and hence they have a pathological character."[44] The ABC of bestialism is that everything is permissible: "Man may be used in any way desired for the attainment of inhuman and antihuman aims."[45] Objectification leads, with reliable regularity, to a denial of the value of the human personality. Man is depersonalized and dehumanized by its operation. He loses his personality and his humanity when he is used as a means for whatever ends. Our modern world is not moved by the values of the spirit, the value of the human personality, the value of human freedom, the value of eternal truth. It is moved by such values as power, wealth, nation, class, race. All these and many others are put above man by man himself. Power ranks high in man's estimation, even higher than his own personality. The quest for power leads him to sacrifice his humanity and thus he becomes inhuman to his fellowman. The process of depersonalization and dehumanization, Berdyaev regretfully declares, has indeed penetrated all phases of human life.

A conspicuous picture of man's dehumanization and the loss of his personal freedom may be observed in the field of economics. Personality is made to depend on what a man possesses. Property is considered the guarantee of man's freedom and security. But the freedom and security conferred by property vanish with the loss of that property.

[44] Berdyaev, *The Fate of Man in the Modern World*, p. 20
[45] *Ibid.*, p. 21

Money, "the great enslaver of a man and of mankind," is "symbol of impersonality."[46]

Berdyaev does not hesitate to pass judgment on both Capitalism and Communism as powerful agents of depersonalization and dehumanization. As an economic system, Capitalism is the breeding of money by money for money's sake. Production exists for the purpose of making profits, and man exists to keep the wheels of production turning. No wonder such a system sees nothing wrong with destroying large quantities of food supplies for purely economic interests at a time when millions are starving. Man does have the duty to develop himself economically, but, Berdyaev cautions,

> The divorce of economy from life, the technical interpretation of life, and the fundamental capitalist principle of profit, transform man's economic life into a fiction. The capitalist system is sowing the seeds of its own destruction by sapping the spiritual foundation of man's economic life.[47]

Berdyaev's verdict on Communism is equally severe, but it takes a different direction. On the whole, he had no economic nor even political quarrels with Communism. He was in favor of its objectives of putting an end to the exploitation of man by man, and of terminating the class struggle and giving birth to a classless society. He commended the communist dream of creating a world organization that would abolish war. But he vigorously opposed both Marxism and Communism on spiritual grounds. In Marxism, he discerned an economic variation of the Hegelian theme. In his book, *The Realm of Spirit and the Realm of Caesar*, Berdyaev devotes a chapter to an analysis of "The Contradictions in Marxism." "The contradiction in Marxism lies also in the fact that the realm of freedom . . . will be the inevitable result of necessity . . . This is

[46] Berdyaev, *Slavery and Freedom*, p. 187
[47] Berdyaev, *The Meaning of History*, p. 219

essentially a denial of freedom."[48] Marx subjected man "to historic necessity, to the point of deifying this necessity."[49] He thought of the present as nothing but means to the future; and thus, as Berdyaev writes, "the value of human life for itself in the present is denied."[50] The system that set out to humanize society produced "a process of dehumanization," for "Marx's atheism . . . results from his exclusion of one very important phase, of man as a spiritual being."[51]

Berdyaev was convinced that today's Communism has deviated from the original economic philosophy of Marxism and has become a form of "State Capitalism." He recognized soon after the Russian Revolution that "Communism . . . imperils the living principle of freedom and personality."[52] In his book, *The Origin of Russian Communism,* Berdyaev has clearly shown how "only that sort of freedom, freedom for the collective construction of life in the general direction of the communist party, is recognized in Soviet Russia."[53] Furthermore, hostility to religion belongs to the very essence of Communism. It denies the freedom of choice and the freedom of conscience and thus it crushes with its materialistic fist man's individual personality and personal liberty. Its denial of God naturally leads to its denial of the human personality.

Having to work with and through machines, man is finding that slowly but surely his emotional life is being damaged. The machines were invented for the purpose of freeing man from slavery to nature and time, and were supposed to lighten the burden of his labor, but instead

[48] Berdyaev, *The Realm of Spirit and the Realm of Caesar,* p. 137 f

[49] *Ibid.,* p. 149

[50] *Ibid.,* p. 147

[51] *Ibid.*

[52] Berdyaev, *Dream and Reality,* p. 241

[53] Berdyaev, *The Origin of Russian Communism,* p. 152

they have become his mute yet noisy slave driver and not infrequently invoke upon him the curse of unemployment. Through the mechanization of life, man is mercilessly forced to degenerate into a machine. Confronted with "almighty technics," man is dissolved into certain functions. His personality, his freedom, his real center, all disappear. Closely related to the towering achievements of modern technology are the amazing discoveries of modern science, which likewise have a hand in the process of dehumanization.

Berdyaev recognizes the symptoms of dehumanization also in modern literature and philosophy. Particularly in the novel, he finds that man is decomposed and that his whole imagination is distorted. His real image can no longer be discerned. In the psychological novel, which is concerned with the analysis of the subconscious life, man appears to be dissolved into one or a few of his component elements. "Modern novelists almost completely lack creative imagination, they are either preoccupied with themselves, or simply picture the evil realities with which they are burdened."[54] Often, the characters disappear beneath their sadistic instincts or are lost in the blind alleys of their sex life. No doubt, admits Berdyaev, the modern novel contains much of the truth about man and about what is happening to him in the present age.

In philosophic thought, the depersonalization and alienation of the human personality is a more complex process. It may be detected in such movements as empiricism, idealism, naturalism and materialism. Modern philosophy, particularly Existentialism, although it stresses the question about man, his existence and freedom, has nevertheless betrayed signs of disintegration and degradation. In Heidegger's ontology of Nothing, Berdyaev finds a philosophy of pessimism and despair in which man is hopelessly

[54] Berdyaev, *The Fate of Man in the Modern World*, p. 28

lost in a metaphysical jungle of fear, worry, and death.[55]
Jaspers, whom Berdyaev regarded as "a far more authentic
existentialist than Heidegger and Sartre,"[56] shows a modi-
fied tendency toward the same thinking as Heidegger[57]
even though he did not admit "an ontological knowledge
by means of concepts" and accepted only "the possibility
of metaphysics as symbolic knowledge."[58] Berdyaev severely criticizes Sartre's philosophy, "which debases man
and denies every higher principle in him," and he wonders
how it "can possibly be linked with the *rôle* of freedom
in human life, and the possibility of creating a new and
better way of life."[59] He finds Sartre's concept of freedom
and his emphasis that "man is condemned to freedom"
too negative, too empty, and devoid of any connection
with truth.[60] And what metaphysics is there in Freud except the metaphysics of death and nothingness? According
to Freud, says Berdyaev, man is torn between the instinct
of sex and the instinct of death.[61] He also mentions the
"dehumanization of Christianity" by some modern religious thinkers such as Karl Barth in whose "dialectic
theology . . . the image of God in man is shattered."[62]

Throughout his books, Berdyaev discusses with existential flavor the dehumanizing operations which are characteristic of "the realm of Caesar," the state. He agrees with
Nietzsche that "the state is the most cold-blooded of
monsters."[63] There is in man a natural disposition to

[55] Berdyaev, *The Fate of Man in the Modern World*, p. 30 f
[56] Berdyaev, *Toward a New Epoch*, p. 97
[57] Berdyaev, *The Fate of Man in the Modern World*, p. 31
[58] Berdyaev, *Toward a New Epoch*, p. 96
[59] *Ibid.*, p. 100
[60] *Ibid.*, pp. 100, 103
[61] Berdyaev, *The Fate of Man in the Modern World*, p. 31
[62] *Ibid.*
[63] Berdyaev, *Slavery and Freedom*, p. 144

dominate others. He finds it hard to resist the temptation to develop and exercise sovereignty over his fellow men.

Unfortunately, says Berdyaev regretfully, Christians have not followed the example of Christ. They have responded to the claims of sovereigns by genuflecting without reflection. The words of Christ "Render unto Caesar the things that are Caesar's and unto God the things that are God's" have commonly been misunderstood and misinterpreted. They have often been taken as a justification for reconciling the kingdom of Caesar and the Kingdom of God. But these words of the Master, Berdyaev explains, do not imply evaluations and do not give Caesar and his realm a religious connotation. They were not meant to abolish the conflict between the two kingdoms.[64] Was not the life of Christ precisely this conflict carried out till the end with earnestness and without flinching?

The clash between the Kingdom of God and the kingdom of Caesar is here to stay because under the conditions of this world the function of the state is necessary. It will always remain so. In philosophical terms, this is the conflict between freedom and necessity, between the spirit and the objectified world. What must be rejected is the state's claim of sovereignty. "Sovereignty belongs to no one: it is only one of the illusions of objectification."[65] Caesar is the product and the agent of the objectified world and therefore cannot hold the right of sovereignty. "The relationships between church and state have been, and always will be, contradictory and they present an insoluble problem."[66]

The tragic fact is that the cult of sovereignty is, nevertheless, practiced in the kind of world we live in, and the

[64] Berdyaev, *The Realm of Spirit and the Realm of Caesar,* p. 69 f

[65] *Ibid.,* p. 71

[66] *Ibid.,* p. 73 f

poison of imperial authority runs in the veins of human rulers. The state itself, especially the totalitarian state, never refrains from attempting, and never gives up pretending, to act as if it were a church in giving meaning to the lives of men, and thus exercises domain over their souls, minds, and hearts. The state has continuously shown the tendency and desire to trespass the limits of control and authority and power to which it is lawfully entitled. The totalitarian state voices and defends the arrogant and erroneous claim that man exists for its own sake. Instead of being the guardian of man's rights and the protector of his freedom, it stamps upon his rights and tramples his temple of freedom. Consequently, man is dehumanized and his personality is paralyzed by the state's hypnotic power. He surrenders his freedom at the altar where the mystifying and stultifying sacrament of imperial authority is administered. Knowingly or unknowingly, the state is inclined to be guided by the expedient principle that prevailed at the trial of Jesus: "It is better for us that one man should die for the people than the whole nation should perish." But Berdyaev is not unaware of the complexity caused by the fact that the people themselves are not always innocent but often find their own deceitful dreams come true in the actions and transactions of the state.

> The state is, of course, a projection, an exteriorization, an objectification of a condition of the people themselves . . . and there lies the chief evil and a source of human slavery.[67]

The greatest threat confronts man, Berdyaev argues, when the state is conceived as a personality, as an organism, having its own existence apart from the people. It is then that its depersonalizing mechanism operates on a larger and more dangerous scale. It is then that "the

[67] Berdyaev, *Slavery and Freedom*, p. 145

prince of this world" is already at the helm of the state steering it to totalitarianism and, with it, to self-destruction. But regardless of the uniform he wears and the flag he flies, Caesar has an irresistable tendency to demand not only what is properly his own, but also what is God's; he wants the whole of man to be subject to himself. And in this lies the greatest tragedy of history, that of freedom and necessity, of human fate and historic destiny.[68]

4 INDIVIDUALISM AND COLLECTIVISM

In individualism and collectivism, Berdyaev discovers two grave enemies of personality and freedom. "Free personality is a flower that blooms but rarely in the life of the world."[69] Individualism, as understood by Berdyaev, destroys it from within, and collectivism from without.

By individualism Berdyaev does not mean what is generally understood by the term, namely, the liberation of the individual from natural and social pressures, and the exercise of independent and original judgment rather than stereotyped conformity to customs and conventions. "If we understand individualism in this fashion, then we must recognize positive value in it."[70] The individualism that Berdyaev has in mind "is opposed to universalism; it is the disunion of the human individuality from the universe; it is self-idolization."[71] Earlier in the same context, he stresses the fact that "individuality and individualism are opposites. Individualism is the enemy of individuality."[72]

[68] Berdyaev, *The Realm of Spirit and the Realm of Caesar*, p. 78 f
[69] Berdyaev, *Slavery and Freedom*, p. 138
[70] Berdyaev, *The Meaning of the Creative Act*, p. 154; cf. Berdyaev, *Slavery and Freedom*, p. 133
[71] Berdyaev, *The Meaning of the Creative Act*, p. 154
[72] *Ibid.*, p. 153

A number of times, Berdyaev defines individualism as a process of "atomization" of society.[73] The term seems to be equated with the lack of "interior unity," when he refers to the nineteenth century which, in his opinion, was "infected by individualism, by 'atomism.' "[74] Berdyaev's definition of individualism is not clear and sounds rather arbitrary. It is possible that for him the term signifies chiefly self-centered non-involvement or isolationism. "The individualist isolates himself and asserts himself in his attitude to the universe."[75]

According to Berdyaev, individualism is diametrically opposed to personalism. "Individualism is a natural philosophy, whereas personalism is a philosophy of the spirit."[76] The same distinction and contrast were made long before him by Yuri F. Samarin (1819–76), one of the leading Slavophiles, who also conceived of the "individual" principle as "a principle of *disunion* rather than union," and of the "individual person" as the "person who makes himself the absolute measure of all things."[77]

For Berdyaev, individualism, that is, egocentric isolationism, the "atomization" of life and society, is a condition that is void of the qualities of free personality. It is the absence of "the affirmation of the supreme value of personality."[78] Through this selfish isolationism man "tries convulsively to free himself from the world, from the cosmos—and attains only slavery; for to separate oneself inwardly from the universe is inevitably to enslave

[73] Berdyaev, *The End of our Time*, pp. 85, 91, 96
[74] *Ibid.*, p. 83
[75] Berdyaev, *Slavery and Freedom*, p. 135
[76] *Ibid.*, p. 138
[77] Zenkovsky, *A History of Russian Philosophy*, Vol. I, p. 230 f
[78] Berdyaev, *Slavery and Freedom*, p. 133

oneself to it outwardly."[79] Man's slavery to his environment is the indirect result of his slavery to himself.[80]

Berdyaev shows how when man dissociates himself from his fellow men and tries to be an independent semi-god, his personality falls apart into separate self-affirming, but mutually contending, intellectual, emotional and sensory elements. The inward core of the personality is broken and the sundered parts seeking to be autonomous tear a person to pieces. Such a man loses the dignity of his personality and the freedom of his spirit. He succumbs to real and imagined fears and anxieties. He ceases to be a free person and becomes a slave to himself.[81]

Man becomes an obedient slave not only of his lower, animal nature, but also, a more disturbing fact, of his higher nature. He has the devious ability to turn the highest values into instruments of selfish goals. Berdyaev cites the Pharisee as an example of this tragic and harmful distortion. In this historic and symbolic figure, devotion and loyalty to the law of goodness and brotherhood were transformed into egocentric self-satisfaction and belligerent self-admiration.[82] In a very strange and often unconscious way, ideas and ideals put themselves or, more correctly, are put by man, at the disposal of his selfish instincts and desires; and this, sooner or later, leads to his self-destruction. All these internal enemies of man's personal freedom frequently masquerade as individualism. "It is remarkable," writes Berdyaev, "that great creative men have in fact never been individualists. They have been solitary and unrecognized, they have been in sharp conflict with their environment . . . they have always thought of themselves as called to serve."[83]

[79] Berdyaev, *The Meaning of the Creative Act*, p. 153
[80] Berdyaev, *Slavery and Freedom*, p. 132
[81] *Ibid.*, p. 135
[82] *Ibid.*, p. 132
[83] *Ibid.*, p. 136

Man is also lured by collectivism which induces him to barter his personality and freedom for a mirage of security. The hypnotic spell of collectivism plays a major role in human life. Man's personality is very much like an intersection where various social groups meet.

Berdyaev refers to Georg Simmel (1858–1918), the German sociologist and social philosopher, who saw in society merely the reciprocal action of individuals. Man belongs to the family, the class, the profession, the club, the nation. These have only a functional relation to him. But as he objectifies his relationship to these groups, they begin to appear to him as independent entities of which he is a subordinate part.[84] In other words, personality is dissolved in its social function. Man ceases to be a supreme value.

"Collectivism," insists Berdyaev, "is a false condition of consciousness which sets up a false reality."[85] What he means is that collective groups are secondary and derivative, rather than primary, realities. They are realities of quite another order than such realities as the human personality. We often speak, for instance, of a collective national consciousness as if the nation as such had a consciousness of its own apart from the people who constitute it. It is a mistake to think of collective groups as having their own existence above and beyond the personalities which form such collectives. A social group does not possess a consciousness of its own apart from the consciousness of all the individuals within it. Berdyaev put the matter briefly and concretely when he wrote:

> The main characteristic of so-called collective realities is that they do not have an existential centre, they can neither suffer nor rejoice.[86]

[84] Berdyaev, *Slavery and Freedom*, p. 201
[85] Berdyaev, *The Realm of Spirit and the Realm of Caesar*, p. 117
[86] *Ibid.*, p. 118

The collective is Martin Heidegger's *das Man*. Because it is impersonal, it is also anti-personal. It does not and cannot recognize the value of personality; and, paradoxically, this is what makes it authoritarian. Berdyaev elucidates this point by saying:

> In it (collectivism) the centre of consciousness and conscience is situated outside personality in massive, collective, social groups, for example in the army or in totalitarian parties. Cadres and parties may reduce the personal consciousness to a state of paralysis.[87]

Berdyaev is by no means consistent here. He denies collective groups consciousness of their own and then he speaks of them as if they had such consciousness. In the preceding quotation, for instance, how could "the centre of consciousness and conscience" be "situated . . . in massive, collective, social groups, for example in the army," if collective groups could not possibly have their own consciousness? Moreover, Berdyaev writes that "we may use collective as an adjective, but not as a noun,"[88] yet, he does not apply this counsel to himself.

Perhaps we may understand more fully what Berdyaev means by the enslaving power of collectivism if we follow the distinction he makes between nation and people, nationalism and patriotism. The *nation* is a product of history and civilization, while the *people* is a much more primary and natural reality. The nation is a principle that dominates human beings and, as such, is abstractly real. The term people is more personal than the nation because it connotes human beings who have personalities. The nation is more intimately related to the idea of the state than people are. Therefore, the concept *nation* indicates a greater degree of objectification and, with it, a greater

[87] Berdyaev, *Slavery and Freedom*, p. 202
[88] Berdyaev, *The Realm of Spirit and the Realm of Caesar*, p. 117

degree of dehumanization than is the case with the term *people*.

Furthermore, a similar distinction exists between nationalism and patriotism. *Nationalism* is a collective egocentricity and the will power over others. *Patriotism* is the love of one's native land, of its soil and people. "Nationalism is an idealized form of the self-exaltation of man."[89] Patriotism as the "love for one's people is a very natural and good feeling."[90] Nationalism leads to tyranny. It absorbs the human personality and humanity alike. One of the causes of man's slavery is that the nation and nationalism give him a greater but deceptive feeling of power. Through objectification, they tend to become idols which claim man's allegiance. Part of the falsity of this objectification is the dangerous belief that evils such as egoism, self-seeking, pride, hatred of others and violence all become virtues when transferred from personality to the nation. When the nation is idolized by man, it demands his unconditional allegiance and relishes above all the sacrifice of his own freedom. "The emotions of nationalism eject man on to the surface and, therefore, make man a slave of the object world."[91]

In this chapter, the process of objectification and its implications for the human personality have been discussed. Figuratively speaking, objectification is a downward movement or, as its synonym *exteriorization* indicates, a movement from within into an outward direction. It is turning things inside out, the converting of a subject into an object. The results of this process are distressing, as Berdyaev sees them. The human personality is deprived of its existential center. Man ceases to be man and loses his freedom and dignity. He is depersonalized and dehu-

---

[89] Berdyaev, *Slavery and Freedom*, p. 165
[90] *Ibid.*
[91] *Ibid.*, p. 172

manized. The being who was created in God's image and was meant to be free has been turned, by his own manipulation as well as by forces beyond his control, into an animal and is placed in the cage of necessity.

But Berdyaev also states that man has not necessarily reached a dead end and that his predicament is not entirely hopeless. There are forces within man that rebel against this condition of slavery. The degrading movement of objectification has its countermovement, which will ultimately lead to man's liberation.

> The first move was in the direction of objectification. The second move must take the opposite direction, towards primary spiritual experience, towards the existential subject, not towards the "natural", but towards the reverse of objectified nature, towards spirituality.[92]

It is to this "second move . . . the opposite direction . . . towards spirituality" that we must turn now, where Berdyaev's philosophy reaches its apex and where, in his opinion, the paradox of freedom and necessity can find its final solution.

[92] Berdyaev, *Truth and Revelation*, p. 67

CHAPTER V

FREEDOM AND CREATIVITY

(The Key to the Solution)

1 THE NATURE OF CREATIVENESS

Berdyaev interprets the New Testament parable of the seed falling on good soil and yielding fruits abundantly, as well as the parable of the talents that are put to use profitably, as references to man's creativity. Burying one's talents in the ground is the absence of creativeness. It is condemned by Christ. To be actively creative is man's vocation. It is his duty and obligation. St. Paul's teaching about various gifts, according to Berdyaev, deals with man's creative activity.

But what is the nature of creativeness? Simply, Berdyaev replies, it is "the making of something new that had not existed before."[1] Creativeness involves growth and change. It is bringing forth something out of nothing. This is creativity in its strictest ontological sense. Nothing becomes something. Non-being becomes being. True creativeness is not evolution, the redistribution of force and energy, but rather revolution, the appearance of something new that never existed before. "Evolution," says Berdyaev, "is necessity, creation is freedom."[2]

Creativeness, in other words, is the absence of determination. Bringing into existence something out of something else is, to Berdyaev's way of thinking, not creative-

[1] Berdyaev, *The Destiny of Man*, p. 126
[2] *Ibid.*

ness, because it involves some degree of determination. Berdyaev equates the absence of determination, this non-being or nothingness, which creativeness presupposes, with freedom itself which he describes as "primeval, pre-cosmic, pre-existent."[3]

For Berdyaev, the belief that God created the world out of nothing means that he created it freely and out of freedom. Creation was not a process of emanation from God. It was a creative activity which brought about a new world that had never existed before, neither actually nor potentially. Accordingly, creativeness means breaking through from non-being, from freedom, to the world of being.[4]

When Berdyaev ascribes the creative activity to man, he does that on the grounds that by virtue of having been created in God's image and likeness, man is a creator and is assigned the duty to engage in creative work.[5] This, however, makes human creativeness a complex fact. Ontologically, we cannot say the same thing about it that we say about divine creativeness.

According to Berdyaev, there are three elements in human creativeness: first, the created world, which is both the source from which man obtains his raw materials, and the workshop in which he creates; second, the gifts, the talents, with which man is endowed by his Creator; third, man's primary freedom which itself, states Berdyaev, is not created. Through his freedom, man applies his given talents of mind to the given world of nature and produces something new. Thus "the creative act is of the nature of marriage, it always implies a meeting between different elements."[6] This we find in all phases of civilization, in inventions, discoveries, in art and philosophy.

[3] Berdyaev, *The Destiny of Man*, p. 127
[4] *Ibid.*
[5] *Ibid.*
[6] *Ibid.*

Berdyaev emphasizes the factor of freedom in human creativeness. Without it there can be no creative activity. What does he mean by this freedom? His answer is merely: "It is, indeed, not 'something' but 'nothing.' "[7] When we say that man creates out of nothing, it means that he creates out of freedom. Without making what he actually means any clearer, Berdyaev admits that "the creative process is so complex that it is not easy to detect this primary element (of 'fathomless freedom') in it."[8]

Viewed chronologically and teleologically, creativeness has two stages, two aspects. There is the inner, primary aspect, which is the creative conception, the creative intuition; and there is the outer, secondary aspect, which is the actual realization, the concrete expression, of what is inwardly conceived. When a creative work, such as a book, a symphony or some architectural design, is being conceived, the creative mind is perfectly free. The conception of any work takes place in the realm of freedom. But the moment the same work enters the second stage of creativeness, namely, its concrete actualization in time and space, it falls under the shadow of necessity, the limitations and pressures caused by the world of beings and things. Precisely because creativeness is not only an ascending movement, conception, intuition, but also a descending movement, realization, actualization, it has a paradoxical and tragic nature. In the words of Berdyaev,

> There is always a tragic discrepancy between the burning heat of the creative fire in which the artistic image is conceived, and the cold of its realization. Every book, picture, statue, good work, social institution is an instance of this cooling down of the original flame.[9]

The distinction between the creative act and the created

7 *Ibid.*, p. 128
8 *Ibid.*
9 *Ibid.*, p. 129

5

product is strictly maintained by Berdyaev. The latter, but not the former, comes under the influence of the process of objectification. The results of creative activity, the cold products of civilization, cultural values, books, paintings, symphonies, buildings, social institutions, and even good works, all come under the spell of necessity. However, the creative act itself, creative inspiration and illumination, creative perception and conception, remain free from objectification. They are beyond time and space. They are subjective and belong to the realm of freedom and eternity. In other words, the creative act has a liberating effect because it involves self-forgetfulness and sacrifice.

The flight into the inner space of creative activity is made on the wings of imagination. "Without imagination there can be no creative activity."[10] Through the eyes of imagination we discern something superior to the reality around us. Imagination has this function not only in art, but also in science as well as ethics. A better life, for instance, must first be imagined before it can be pursued. Of course, Berdyaev does not mean here legalistic ethics, which he vehemently abhors. No imagination is needed if we think of morality in terms of obedience to the law. Sure enough, we can imagine the consequences of our obeying or disobeying, but our response to the law itself, whether positive or negative, requires no imaginative projection. Legalistic ethics is very different from what Berdyaev calls "the ethics of creativeness," which will be discussed later. There imagination is indispensable and plays the role of talent. A person without the power of imagination is incapable of creative activity. He cannot improve his ethical life, since he is unable to imagine a better life than the one he leads.

> By the side of the self-contained moral world of laws and rules . . . man builds in imagination a higher, free and beauti-

[10] Berdyaev, *The Destiny of Man*, p. 142

ful world beyond ordinary good and evil. And this is what gives beauty to life.[11]

2   CREATIVITY AND ETHICS

Berdyaev distinguishes three levels of ethical standard and moral conduct. The lowest is the "ethics of law"[12] which rules in all pre-Christian morality. This is deeply imbedded in society and could be traced to tribal life. Martin Luther, for instance, protested against the legalistic ethics of the Roman Catholic Church. The ethics of law is essentially social and gives expression to herd morality. It may also be found disguised in a philosophical uniform, and claim to be based on freedom and autonomy. The ethics of law poses as normative and idealistic. This is true of Kantian morality, which, despite its emphasis on freedom and autonomy, is legalistic inasmuch as it is concerned with the universally binding law. "Individuality does not exist for Kantian ethics, any more than do unique and individual moral problems which demand unique and individual, i.e. creative, moral solutions."[13]

The ethics of law promises happiness as a result of obedience to the law. But such happiness is never genuine, as it ignores man's right of free creation of spiritual values. It conflicts with man's fundamental freedom. However, the ethics of law is necessary to man in his fallen state. It is necessary to all who live in slavery because they know no other morality. Society needs the ethics of law because it is made of "natural" men who are not "redeemed." Legalistic restraints and implements are necessary in the world with its objectified condition. But we must keep in mind, says Berdyaev, that man cannot be saved by the law of morality because it demands obedience and not free creative activity. "Man is not a passive executor of the laws

[11] *Ibid.*, p. 143
[12] *Ibid.*, pp. 84-102
[13] *Ibid.*, p. 97

. . . Man is a creator and an inventor . . . Life is based upon energy and not upon law."[14]

Furthermore, there is the "ethics of redemption."[15] Redemption is the message of liberation proclaimed by Christianity. The Redeemer is the Liberator. Christ did what the law could not do, namely, regenerate man and set him free from the grip of fear and guilt. The ethics of redemption is based on, and issues from, this spiritual experience. It rests on existence and life and not on norm and law. The radical revolution of Christianity may be expressed in the words of Christ: "The Sabbath is made for man and not man for the Sabbath." The ethics of redemption is man-centered and not law-centered. Its primary consideration is man. It is an ethics of love and freedom, Berdyaev points out. Christian love is concrete and personal. Personality has a supreme value as the image of God. This applies also to the personality of the enemy, who must equally be the object of our love. The note of freedom in the Christian ethics of redemption is unmistakably heard. Man must be inwardly free under all circumstances. "Where the Spirit of the Lord is (the Spirit of love and compassion), there is liberty." The true Christian finds that his ethical standard is diametrically opposed to the standard of the world.

Berdyaev develops a third type of ethics which he designates as "the ethics of creativeness."[16] This is concerned not with salvation, as it is the case with the ethics of redemption, but rather with the creation of values. Though the ethics of creativeness springs from the personality, it is concerned with society and the world. It affirms the value of the unique and the particular. In Berdyaev's opinion, as already indicated, all moral valuations

[14] Berdyaev, *The Destiny of Man*, p. 133
[15] *Ibid.*, pp. 103–25
[16] *Ibid.*, pp. 126–53

must proceed from the personality and be unique in character. Personality itself is the highest value and must always be treated as an end in itself and never as a means to another end. "Personality is the only truly creative and prophetic element in moral life, it coins new values. But it suffers for doing so."[17]

The ethics of creativeness seeks to transform the world through creative acts which give meaning to life. It certainly does not contradict the ethics of redemption in doing so; on the contrary, it presupposes and supplements it. The redeemed man wants to exercise his creative powers because God works partly through him. Creation is never complete. We are living in "the eighth day of creation."

> The ethics of creativeness calls for actual, concrete realization of truth, goodness, spirituality, for a real transfiguration of life and not for a symbolic and conventional realization of the good through ascetic practices, good works and so on.[18]

Through concentrated and self-forgetful creativity, man frees himself from the shackles of necessity. Through the creative act man is rescued from the evil of lusts and passions, which are transfigured into noble qualities. He breaks the bondage to time and space with their pressing limitations. The creative work does occur in time and space, but the creative act itself is part of eternity and is directed toward beauty, truth, and eternal values. Berdyaev identifies creativeness with Christian love:

> All creativeness is love and all love is creative. If you want to receive, give, if you want to obtain satisfaction, do not seek it, never think of it and forget the very word; if you want to acquire strength, manifest it, give it to others.[19]

The mystery of life is that satisfaction is felt not by those who take and make demands but by those who give and make

[17] *Ibid.*, p. 135
[18] *Ibid.*, p. 139
[19] *Ibid.*, p. 141

sacrifices. In them alone the energy of life does not fail, and this is precisely what is meant by creativeness. Therefore the positive mystery of life is to be found in love, in sacrificial, giving, creative love.[20]

3 THE PURPOSE OF ART

The meaning of the creative act is best revealed in artistic expressions. To be an artist is to be a creator. The artist deals with the world of beauty, which discloses itself in our own world. But the artistic activity may also take the form of contemplation which is by no means passivity, as many would say, but activity. Contemplation, Berdyaev believes, "comprises a distinctly active and creative element."[21] This does not apply only to artistic contemplation but to contemplation in general. This is reminiscent of Aristotle who considered theoretical contemplation as an activity—the highest and best in which man can engage and the source of his greatest happiness, an activity that includes artistic imagination and creativity.[22] The appreciation of beauty, according to Berdyaev, is in itself an activity.[23] "Contemplation of natural beauty is more than a state: it is an act, a breaking through to another world."[24] The reception of beauty involves a creative activity within man through which he experiences a temporary liberation from the determinism of this world. "Beauty, like truth, is in subjectivity, not in objectivity."[25] "Accepting the beauty in the world unto oneself is always

[20] Berdyaev, *The Destiny of Man*, p. 141

[21] Berdyaev, *Dream and Reality*, p. 220

[22] Aristotle, *Nichomachean Ethics*, Book X, Chapt. 7-8, trans. by W. D. Ross in Richard McKeon (ed.), *The Basic Works of Aristotle* (New York: Random House, 1941), pp. 1104-8

[23] Berdyaev, *The Meaning of the Creative Act*, p. 225

[24] Berdyaev, *Dream and Reality*, p. 220

[25] Berdyaev, *Slavery and Freedom*, p. 242

creativity."[26] This is so whether or not it leads to concrete artistic creation. The liberation that is experienced through beauty, this "break-through" into another world, "takes place in every creative act of art and in every artistic reception of that creative act."[27] Artistic contemplation and appreciation are themselves a creative activity, even though they may not result in artistic productions, because they involve "a judgment of taste." "The beautiful pleases, not in its reception by the senses, not in a concept, but in an act of judgment, in appraisal."[28]

Berdyaev warns against confusing this creative artistic receptivity with the experience of "people who live under the spell of beauty and art." Such people have surrendered to what he calls "the aesthetic lure,"[29] which is "the lure of passivity." "The aesthetic type" is merely a consumer of art, an observer, in the sense that, lacking any subjectivity, his reaction to art is limited to his emotions. He is conscious of the phenomenal world and the products of artistic creativity, but has no awareness of, and no contact with, the world of the spirit and the creative activity of which it is a part. "An exclusively aesthetic orientation to life enfeebles the sense of reality."[30] It weakens and even destroys the value of personality because it displaces its existential center and turns one part of man, his feelings and emotions, into a whole.

In Berdyaev's opinion, when this superficial conception and reception of art, which he designates as "aestheticism" as contrasted with real art, invades the artistic area of man's life, it has the tendency, like an infection, to spread to all aspects of life. In religion, it appears in the form

26 Berdyaev, *The Meaning of the Creative Act*, p. 225
27 Berdyaev, *Slavery and Freedom*, p. 241
28 Berdyaev, *The Beginning and the End*, p. 191
29 Berdyaev, *Slavery and Freedom*, p. 237
30 *Ibid.*, p. 239

of the predominance of liturgy. In morality, aestheticism substitutes personal attractiveness for virtue. In philosophy, it finds expression in an exaggerated preoccupation with a certain emotional condition, depending on the aesthetic type, and an utter disregard for truth. In politics, it ignores the cause of justice and freedom and focuses attention on an idealized past or an idealized future or both.[31] "The aesthetic lure," says Berdyaev, "reminds us of magic." It is seductive, deceptive, hypnotizes especially the masses, and inevitably leads to the dissolution of personality.

Unlike "aesthetics," art and beauty are liberating in their creativeness. They elevate us to another plane of existence by achieving a break-through in this world of objectification and determinism. As a creative activity, art is not adaptation to this world but rather victory over it.

> In art there is liberation. The essential in artistic creativity is victory over the burden of necessity. In art man lives outside himself, outside his burdens, the burden of life. Every creative artistic act is a partial transfiguration of life.[32]
>
> Creativeness in art, like every other form of creative activity, consists in triumph over given, determined, concrete life, it is a victory over the world.[33]

Through artistic creativity, a transformation of matter takes place. A shapeless stone becomes a beautiful statue, and a chaos of sounds is cast into a great symphony. All the great artists, each in his way, have been conquerors of the burden and resistance of matter and necessity. Richard Wagner, for instance, attempted to overcome necessity by transforming life through a synthesis of music and poetry. Berdyaev considers music the most dynamic of all arts and the most powerful in its influence upon the

[31] Berdyaev, *Slavery and Freedom*, p. 238
[32] Berdyaev, *The Meaning of the Creative Act*, p. 225
[33] Berdyaev, *The Beginning and the End*, p. 173

soul. "Beethoven was a prophet,"[34] he writes. His music gave expression particularly to the tragedy of man. The music of Bach, on the other hand, sought to express "the music of the heavenly spheres."[35] The experience of beauty through drama such as a tragedy, as Aristotle had shown, brings about a catharsis and liberation. Tragic suffering has this purifying and emancipating effect "because between our suffering and tragedy and the suffering and tragedy in the productions of art lies a transfiguring, creative artistic act."[36]

Art liberates man from slavery to everyday life because its creative activity issues from the subjective spirit and is, therefore, spiritual.[37] "Art is religious in the depths of the very artistic creative act."[38] However and unfortunately so, this cannot ever be completely the case with the works of art themselves. This is so, says Berdyaev, because "the creative act of spirit is both an ascent and a descent."[39] The creative activity elevates man above the world and liberates him from its necessity, "but the gravity of the world also pulls it down and makes it conform in its products to the state of the world."[40] The works of art are subject to the law of necessity. They must have definite forms. "Without form there is no beauty . . . The creative force of life ought to receive form."[41] The objective world makes art symbolical. "The final reality of beauty is accessible to us in this world only symbolically, only in

34 Berdyaev, *The Meaning of the Creative Act*, p. 250
35 Berdyaev, *The Divine and the Human*, p. 145
36 Berdyaev, *Slavery and Freedom*, p. 241
37 Berdyaev, *Spirit and Reality*, p. 56
38 Berdyaev, *The Meaning of the Creative Act*, p. 248
39 Berdyaev, *Spirit and Reality*, p. 57; cf. Berdyaev, *The Destiny of Man*, p. 129
40 Berdyaev, *Spirit and Reality*, p. 57
41 Berdyaev, *The Divine and the Human*, p. 142

the form of symbols."[42] Berdyaev speaks of the "tragic
discrepancy" that exists between the artistic conception,
the creative activity itself, and its "formal realization."[43]
The "inner aspect" of creativeness is liberating, but the
"outer aspect" is confining. "Creative *works* are within
time, with its objectifications, discords and divisions, but
the creative *act* is beyond time: it is wholly within, subjective, prior to all objectification."[44]

It is necessary to point out in this connection that symbolism has a major function in Berdyaev's philosophy. Reality is created in art through symbols only. This is true of
all culture, which cannot but be symbolic. What is created is not being itself, reality itself, but signs, symbols of
being, of reality. This is an inescapable limitation imposed on all creative activity. In this sense, "symbolism
points up the eternal tragedy of human creativeness, the
great distance which separates artistic creativeness from
the final reality of being."[45] Seen from another viewpoint,
symbolism is "the strength of art" because it serves as a
bridge across the gulf that separates the creative act from
final reality.[46] Symbolism thus enables creative activity
to be a power "to carry on the creation of the world" and
to "anticipate" and "prepare for" its transfiguration.[47]
"This is the meaning of art," says Berdyaev, "of art of any
kind."[48] In *The Meaning of the Creative Act*, Berdyaev
writes: "Art always teaches us that everything passing and
temporal is a symbol of another form of being, permanent
and eternal."[49] This positive role of symbolism as the be-

[42] Berdyaev, *The Meaning of the Creative Act*, p. 246
[43] Berdyaev, *The Destiny of Man*, p. 129
[44] Berdyaev, *Dream and Reality*, p. 220
[45] Berdyaev, *The Meaning of the Creative Act*, p. 239
[46] *Ibid.*
[47] Berdyaev, *The Beginning and the End*, pp. 174, 192
[48] *Ibid.*, p. 174
[49] Berdyaev, *The Meaning of the Creative Act*, p. 238 f

ginning of the road toward freedom will be discussed in
the next chapter.

Berdyaev writes briefly about "symbolism" as a tendency
in modern art. In it he discerns the paradox of a great
creative intensity and indications of the crisis in art and all
culture.[50] In symbolic art there is a refusal to adapt to
this world and a striving beyond the boundaries of traditional art. The "new symbolism" gives expression to "a
thirst for liberation" from bondage to the objectified
world. As such, it marks a transition to a new type of creativeness. "The artistic achievements of the new art are not
as great as are its searching and its suffering."[51] Berdyaev
recognizes the crisis of art in our times particularly in cub-
ism and futurism. Advertising and charlatanry have destroyed the art of our century. Nevertheless, underneath
"this scum" there is something very profound. In the cub-
ism of Picasso, for instance, Berdyaev sees "something
very significant and deeply moving." "In Picasso's pictures,"
he goes on to say, "we feel the real pain of the world's
coming apart, layer by layer, the world's dematerialization
and decrystallization, the atomization of the world's flesh,
the rending of all the veils."[52]

Man's creative activity is not itself the solution to the
paradox of freedom and necessity, but it is an important
step toward that solution. In spite of the limitations that
are imposed upon it in this world of phenomena by the
laws of necessity, it continues to serve a high purpose and
to provide man with meaning and power. "Without it man
would be unable to endure the conditions of his existence
in this world, or to improve those conditions."[53]

[50] *Ibid.*, pp. 240, 243
[51] *Ibid.*, p. 243
[52] *Ibid.*, p. 242
[53] Berdyaev, *The Beginning and the End*, p. 193

4   THE ROLE OF PHILOSOPHY

In the operations of liberating man from the dominion of necessity, philosophy plays a significant role. To clear the stage for this role, Berdyaev strongly criticizes modern philosophy's hope and effort to become scientific. Philosophy is the mother of sciences, and its attempt to become scientific is similar to that of a mother trying to be like her daughter.

The repeated attempts of many philosophers to make philosophy not so much a science but rather *scientific* have serious implications. Berdyaev draws a sharp distinction between science and the scientific. Our need for science cannot be questioned. But the *scientific* is set in the balance and is found wanting. "The scientific means carrying the criteria of science over into other spheres of spiritual life quite foreign to science."[54] Forcing philosophy to apply the methodology of science would be depriving it of its freedom as a sphere of the spiritual life, as an independent domain of culture. Whoever strives to accomplish that is secretly or openly entertaining the conviction that science is the supreme criterion of the whole of life, and to have such a belief in the absolute value and universal application of science is both erroneous and dangerous.

> The scientific—not science—is bondage of the spirit to the lower spheres of being, the constant and ubiquitous consciousness of the power of necessity, of dependence upon the things of this world. It is only one of the ways of expressing the loss of freedom of the creative spirit.[55]

Berdyaev's analysis of the function of science as compared with philosophy is penetrating.[56] Science is man's response to his urge for self-preservation. It is a means of

[54] Berdyaev, *The Meaning of the Creative Act*, p. 24
[55] *Ibid.*, p. 25
[56] *Ibid.*, p. 24 ff

adaptation to the given world with its laws of necessity. Science is knowledge of and out of necessity. It is an agency of orientation in the realm of necessity. "Science is obedience to necessity. Science is not creativity but obedience; its element is not freedom but necessity."[57]

Science, according to Berdyaev, never was nor will be an instrument of man's liberation from the burden of necessity. It will continue to be an expression of his constraint beneath that burden. The category of necessity will never cease to be a fundamental category of scientific thinking. "Science has no vision of freedom in the world."[58] It knows truths but not the Truth. It is a practical adaptation to the objectified world and obedience to its necessity. It covers only one segment of reality, and its laws and methods cannot be universal in their application.

Philosophy, on the other hand, is not limited in its scope of operation. It is a broad and general orientation to the whole of being, seeking the truth about everything and not merely partial truths. Philosophy does not aim at adaptation to necessity. On the contrary, its goal is the liberation of the human spirit from bondage to necessity. It seeks freedom by means of freedom. There may be a philosophy of science, but never a science of philosophy. "To subject philosophy to science is to subject freedom to necessity."[59] "Philosophy is creativeness and not adaptation or obedience."[60]

No doubt, philosophy is in principle a reaction to the world, but it is a reaction which differs from that of science in both its quality and direction. Philosophy is an art rather than a science. It is an art of knowing. Philosophy is creation and not adaptation. It creates ideas which re-

[57] *Ibid.,* p. 26 f
[58] *Ibid.,* p. 26
[59] *Ibid.,* p. 28
[60] *Ibid.,* p. 29

sist the world of necessity by penetrating into the ultimate essence of the world.

It is a truism that, compared with science, philosophy was never as necessary for the preservation of life because it is not economic in its purpose. Berdyaev thinks "there is something of the holiday in philosophy."[61] Nevertheless, man has always needed philosophy to penetrate beyond the visible world. He needs a philosophical vision to see and make sense out of the senselessness of what he sees, the objectified world of necessity. By its basic assumption that there is a meaning to life and that man has the potential to discover that meaning, philosophy has given man the hope and courage to continue his earthly struggle.

> Every age has known its heroes of philosophy, men who defended free philosophy as the art of creating essential ideas through which freedom might be glimpsed beyond necessity and meaning beyond meaninglessness.[62]

Indeed, the whole history of philosophy may be viewed as another arena of the conflict between freedom and necessity, between creativity and adaptation. The philosophers who have tried and are trying today to baptize philosophy in scientific streams are, in Berdyaev's judgment, priests chanting at the altar of necessity. Materialism is the extreme type of philosophy which has bowed its knee to Baal, the god of necessity, who demands obedience and submission. Pragmatism and positivism are noted satellites of necessity's iron rule.

In Bergsonian philosophy, Berdyaev finds the type of pragmatic thinking which "strives creatively to escape the grip of scientific necessity and the shackles of rationalism."[63] Henri Bergson (1859–1940), in his attempt to refute mechanistic materialism and dogmatic naturalism,

[61] Berdyaev, *The Meaning of the Creative Act*, p. 29
[62] *Ibid.*
[63] *Ibid.*, p. 39

developed a philosophy in which he conceived of ultimate reality, the basic *élan vital* (vital impetus) of the universe, in terms of duration and change. Duration is the *thing-in-itself* which can be grasped only by intuition. Bergson gave the free will and the free act primacy over the intellect and being.[64] In opposition to the determinists, who materialize the life of the spirit, he argued that it is not necessarily the strongest motive that always determines our free choice. He stressed the fact that the various courses of action from which we choose are merely possibilities and not "ready-made" alternatives and that it is the will that makes one of them actual. Therefore, Bergson concluded, we are not required by one of the alternate possibilities to choose it as our course of action, simply because the possibility is not an actuality and cannot, therefore, exercise a determining power on us. The weakness of Bergson's line of argument, as Jacques Maritain has clearly shown, lies in its failure to recognize a "psychological causality" and "that it is by reason of the powers (not of phenomena) of the will and intellect (not "motives" and states of consciousness) that the problem should be posited and dealt with."[65] Maritain is right in concluding that "although Bergsonian philosophy has abandoned being and the intellect, in so doing it has not saved freedom, *libertas a necessitate,* such as the testimony of consciousness affirms it."[66] As Berdyaev put it, Bergson's philosophy is on the borderline between necessity and freedom but its face is toward freedom. It is struggling to free

[64] Henri Bergson, *Time and Free Will,* trans. by F. L. Pogson (New York: The Macmillan Co., 1910), Fifth Edition, pp. 165–70, 235–40

[65] Jacques Maritain, *Bergsonian Philosophy and Thomism,* trans. by Mabelle L. Andison (New York: Philosophical Library, 1955), p. 265

[66] *Ibid.*

itself but is not yet free.[67] In Berdyaev's estimate, Bergson did not clearly discern the distinction between philosophy and science. His thinking is still chained to biology, and his "'creative evolution' is altogether a misconception, because creativity and evolution are mutually exclusive notions,"[68] the former belonging to the world of freedom and the latter to the realm of necessity.

Berdyaev advocates a philosophy of freedom and personalism which is a conscious and conscientious rebellion against the captivity of necessity. Its very nature is creative and transforming. It is a free philosophy which repeatedly involves choice and decision. "The true philosopher is a man in love, he who has chosen the object of his knowing love."[69] The task of personalist philosophy, in Berdyaev's opinion, "is to find the most perfect formulation of truth, perceived in intuition, and to synthesize formulae."[70] "These carry conviction," he continues, "by the light which shines out from them, rather than by demonstration or conclusion."[71]

Logical proof, Berdyaev argues, is not necessary because it can prove no truth. Philosophic knowledge involves a high degree of spiritual communication, and it is in that, rather than in books and schools that the sources of philosophy lie. Genuine philosophy has immediate and constant connection with being. It is vitally in touch with life. This is the reason that it should not and cannot be systematic. If it does become systematic, then this is an indication that it has lost its genuineness and degenerated into adaptation to necessity. It can no longer be free. It has defected and has slipped behind the iron curtain of necessity.

[67] Berdyaev, *The Meaning of the Creative Act*, p. 39 f
[68] Berdyaev, *Dream and Reality*, p. 217
[69] Berdyaev, *The Meaning of the Creative Act*, p. 46
[70] *Ibid.*, p. 48
[71] *Ibid.*

The characteristic mark of free philosophy is its creative intuition, and its being "the creative power of man dominating the world."[72] Free philosophy is creative philosophy, and creative philosophy presupposes a creator and his purpose. Therefore, it is anthropocentric. The true philosophy is revealed by man himself. It is an art and not a science. And as a free and creative art, philosophy elevates man through intuitive contemplation and communion with the spiritual world to the heights of true freedom. To liberate him from the prison of necessity and transport him to the frontiers of freedom is the role of creative philosophy.

Being deeply concerned with man's inner life, philosophy, to which Berdyaev subscribes, is committed to the task of investigating all problems from the standpoint of human knowledge. The fact that the knowing subject, through the process of intellection, transforms the object into knowledge, is an evidence of his inherent activity. The process of intellection is essentially creative inasmuch as it discovers meaning beneath the meaningless surface of life and the universe. Through the exercise of his faculties of creation and application, man is helped toward the goal of becoming the master of his world.

In the light of personalistic philosophy, Berdyaev believes, knowledge is both active and creative. "It can illuminate the objective world wherein meaning is revealed, the meaning of human existence and of the universe as a part of the Divine Being."[73] But whenever meaning is revealed, it is inevitably the product of spiritual activity.

It must be borne in mind that in the natural sciences, creative activity is limited by mathematical laws and the information thus acquired is confined to the objectified world. In philosophy, however, creative activity is engaged

[72] *Ibid.*, p. 51
[73] Berdyaev, *Solitude and Society*, p. 53

in discovering the meaning of existence. William James
said that knowledge is not the result of an act, but is itself
an act; and he is right, Berdyaev thinks. "Indeed, it could
not be otherwise since knowledge is a spiritual emanation."[74] Intuition, through which the emanation is channeled, is an active process. Intuition postulates creative inspiration and gives birth to meaning.

Berdyaev brings into the picture the truth scored and
underscored by Wilhelm Dilthey to the effect that thinking is a function of life.

> The whole man, not reason, constructs metaphysics; it is
> not the autonomy of the intellect which needs to be asserted,
> but the autonomy of spirit, the autonomy of the knowing per-
> son as a complete being.[75]

Thinking is part of the person who thinks, and the two
cannot be separated. Intuitive thinking is a creative activity, not a passive reflection. The knowledge acquired by
intuitive thinking is a creative penetration into meaning.
It is wrong to think of metaphysics as a strictly objective
science, Berdyaev points out. Metaphysics is in the thinking subject; and the thinking subject creates spiritual values. Accordingly, metaphysics is empirical because it is
based on spiritual experience. It is a representation of that
experience.

The point must be stressed that Berdyaev conceives of
philosophical knowledge as the knowledge of truth and
not of being. It is the knowledge of what is true and right.
It is a spiritual ascent, an entering into truth. Therefore,
it depends upon the spiritual condition of the subject. In
other words, philosophical knowledge is personal in character. The meaning of the world is found in the subject,
that is, in human existence.[76]

[74] Berdyaev, *Solitude and Society*, p. 53
[75] Berdyaev, *The Beginning and the End*, p. 37
[76] *Ibid.*, p. 40

Philosophical knowledge does not only create values and meanings, but considers it also within its scope of responsibility to bring order and sense into the existing scale of values. This is another way of saying that it endeavors to strive toward a perfect free life. By its very nature, knowledge in general and philosophical knowledge in particular is a liberating agent. To set man free from the power of the objectified world is its domain and its task. Its launching force lies not in the will to power but in the will to meaning and to freedom. Its goal is "the knowledge of truth, the discovery of meaning; its purpose is to give an intelligible sense to reality."[77] But what is the truth which we seek to know? Once this question is raised, we find that philosophy and religion converge, that they are interrelated in a dynamic way.

Berdyaev is not so much interested in knowing reality itself as the truth about it. The place in which this truth may be located is not the object known but the knowing subject, because it is not related to the phenomenal world but to the noumenal world. According to Berdyaev,

> Truth has two meanings. There is truth in the sense of knowledge of reality and there is truth which is reality itself. Truth is not only an idea, and a value, it is also an entity, something which exists. "I am the Truth", . . . Truth is a creative act of spirit in which meaning is brought to birth.[78]

Personality is created by meaning, by truth. It is in this sense that truth is a power which brings about victory over objectification. The knowledge of truth makes men free.

In conclusion, it may be pointed out that Berdyaev's classification of his own philosophy is revealed in his reference to Dilthey's three types of philosophical world outlook: naturalism, objective idealism and idealism of freedom. Berdyaev says: "I should decidedly be placed in the

[77] *Ibid.*, p. 42
[78] *Ibid.*, p. 43

class of idealism of freedom."[79] This position he also calls "realism of freedom." Berdyaev defines his philosophy as that "of the subject, of spirit, of freedom; as being dualistically pluralist, creatively dynamic, personalist and eschatological."[80]

In his autobiography, Berdyaev writes:

I discovered in philosophy a source of freedom[81] . . . I regard my type of philosophy as "existentialist"[82] . . . My philosophy has never been "scientific": rather, it was prophetic and eschatological in manner and orientation.[83]

[79] Berdyaev, *The Beginning and the End*, p. 50
[80] *Ibid.*, p. 51
[81] Berdyaev, *Dream and Reality*, p. 88
[82] *Ibid.*, p. 93
[83] *Ibid.*, p. 91

CHAPTER VI

FREEDOM AND SPIRITUALITY
(The Solution)

1   THE FUNCTION OF SYMBOLISM

In symbolism, Berdyaev recognizes a key with which man can unlock the first gate of his prison of necessity and thus make his initial step toward freedom. No doubt there are other gates, and some can be opened only from the outside. But before one can proceed any further, it is important to comprehend the function of symbolism, which is primary in the spiritual operations of man's liberation.

What is meant by symbol and symbolism? As was hinted in the previous chapter, a symbol signifies a representation of another reality. It is a sign that stands for something else. It suggests a relationship between itself as a sign and the other thing or reality for which it stands. A symbol presupposes the existence of two orders of being and points out the fact that the meaning of the one lies in the other. "A symbol constitutes a bridge which links together two worlds . . . While delimiting both worlds, it also unites them to one another."[1]

The relation between the spiritual world and the natural world, between the realm of freedom and the realm of necessity, states Berdyaev, may be conceived in three different ways: dualistically, monistically and symbolically.[2] The dualistic conception sets God over against the

---

[1] Berdyaev, *Freedom and the Spirit*, p. 52
[2] *Ibid.*, p. 62 f

world and denies any relation between the two. It gives rise to agnostic *positivism* and to *psychologism* in philosophy. The monistic conception of the world considers the realities of the natural world as absolute. It is a rationalism which produces naturalism and materialism. Both of these conceptions, the dualistic and the monistic, separate man from the spiritual world and confine him to the world of physical phenomena, the realm of necessity. They reject the possibility of any relation between the two worlds and insist that between them there can be no interaction, transaction or transfusion. In other words, the world of the spirit and the world of nature are not on speaking terms, and they will never be.

Over against these two conceptions Berdyaev sets and upholds the third, the symbolic conception of the world. Symbolism places the center of gravity of life in the spiritual realm and refuses to see any final reality in the world of phenomena. Yet it admits the possibility of transfusion of spiritual meaning into this world. Berdyaev stresses the conviction that the mystery of the spiritual realm can be expressed only through symbolism and yet it is through symbolism that its distinction from, and close association with, the natural world can be maintained.[3]

To conceive of the natural world symbolically means to discern the spiritual realities behind physical phenomena. In symbols we glimpse the reflection of the invisible world of spiritual realities. As an excellent description of true symbolism, Berdyaev cites the words of St. Paul: "For now we see through a glass darkly, but then face to face; now I know in part, but then shall I know even as also I am known."[4] Only by means of symbolism is the spiritual life perceived in this world.

Furthermore, the meaning of tangible things can be

[3] Berdyaev, *Freedom and the Spirit*, p. 63
[4] I Corinthians 13:12

grasped only by an appeal to the spiritual world. The appeal is made, and the meaning is conveyed, through the symbol, the tangible thing itself. Man's natural life is devoid of meaning without a symbolic interpretation. Such interpretation is liberating in its influence. It recognizes in everything material a symbol of the spiritual, a sign of greater spirituality in relation to the world and of greater freedom from the world. To be aware of the fact that all things in this world are symbols of spiritual realities is to be free from oppressive dependence on this world; "it is to perceive the purpose underlying an otherwise meaningless world."[5]

Symbolization is a reversal of the process of objectification. It is "a return of the objective world to the sphere of inner existence."[6] Symbolization provides us with signs and posters on the highway of life, so to speak, which direct us to the right destination and the proper accommodation. The signs and posters at the roadside stand for something that is elsewhere. Similarly, the symbols we constantly encounter in the objectified world represent meanings in the spiritual world. Unfortunately, we often fall into the temptation of mistaking these symbols for the spiritual realities they denote. It is possible to live under this false impression. As a result, the symbolic value of the phenomenal world disappears and the true spiritual reality is entirely concealed from us. Therefore, warns Berdyaev, it is of utmost importance to grasp the truth that symbolization "is not realization, though there are in it reflections of another world and it foreshows the transfiguration of this world."[7]

Symbolization counteracts objectification, which is a process of adaptation and assimilation to the conditions of

[5] Berdyaev, *Spirit and Reality*, p. 64
[6] *Ibid.*
[7] Berdyaev, *Truth and Revelation*, p. 146

the phenomenal world. Symbolization is the reversal of the estrangement caused by objectification, the force that chains men to the heavy weights of necessity in this world. As such, it is the beginning—but only the beginning—of the process of spiritualization or *subjectification*.

2   THE SIGNIFICANCE OF MYSTICISM

If symbolism is the first stage of liberation from objectification and necessity, mysticism is the second and more important stage. In Berdyaev's judgment, "mysticism is the soil on which religion flourishes and without which it withers and decays."[8] It is the spiritual orbit into which the soul enters and through which it receives the light of revelation. Mysticism is the spiritual illumination that begins with purification and ends with contemplation. It is "a revelation of revelations, a revelation of the realities behind symbols."[9]

At the heart of mysticism is an inner affinity between the divine spirit and the human, between the Creator and the creature. Consequently, mysticism is always concerned with the immanence rather than with the transcendence of God. The immanence is actually experienced, mystics have always claimed. In the mystical experience the dualism between the natural and the supernatural, between the creature and the Creator, disappears. "Mysticism is the overcoming of creatureliness (*Kreaturlichkeit*)."[10]

The liberating quality in mysticism lies in its inwardness and immunity to objectification. Through the mystical experience, man is lifted to high altitudes of spiritual freedom away from the natural and the historical. "Final reality," Berdyaev asserts, "is only revealed in mysticism, in which man escapes from the secondary world of reflections

[8] Berdyaev, *Freedom and the Spirit*, p. 239
[9] Berdyaev, *Spirit and Reality*, p. 119
[10] Berdyaev, *Freedom and the Spirit*, p. 243

and symbols."[11] Although it presupposes a symbolical conception of the world, mysticism abandons symbols and turns to realities.

Berdyaev refers to the conflict between mysticism and theology and attributes it to the fact that mystical experience cannot be translated into theological terminology. The mystical experience is not intended for ordinary communication and it defies the laws of reasoning. Its meaning is distorted whenever it is rendered into the language of theology and metaphysics. The confrontation and experience of the transcendental that occurs in mysticism cannot be rationally expressed. The mystics never felt that their inner experience needed any logical demonstration. They were convinced that the union with God they experienced in their innermost center could not be communicated. If their language betrays an attitude of self-deification it is because the union with God in the inner "castle" of the soul was very real to them. Indeed, some mystics like Meister Eckhart and Angelus Silesius believed not only that they could not exist without God but also that God could not exist without them.[12] In one of his sermons, Eckhart says: "You are a thousand times more necessary to him than he (God) is to you."[13] It would be helpful, Berdyaev suggests, to remember that the expression of mysticism is founded on love rather than on abstract thinking. The mystic's language, for instance, in which he expresses the interdependence of man and God should not be taken literally. It is his manner of stressing the reciprocal love relationship between God and man. As the loved cannot exist without the lover, so also the lover,

[11] *Ibid.*, p. 248

[12] Berdyaev, *Spirit and Reality*, p. 121 f

[13] Eckhart, *Et cum factus esset, Jesus*, p. 121, trans. and quoted in Richard Kroner, *Speculation and Revelation in the Age of Christian Philosophy* (Philadelphia: The Westminster Press, 1959), p. 233 f

God, cannot exist without the loved, man. No doubt, this emphasis can be confusing and misleading to him who is not genuinely mystical.

Berdyaev recognizes that there are types of mysticism that are not necessarily good, such as the kind in which the spiritual and the psychic elements are confused, or the variety in which the spiritual is completely absorbed by the psychic.

There are, in Berdyaev's opinion, two ways of looking at mysticism. On the one hand, "it may be regarded as a peculiarly differentiated form of the spiritual life and as its crowning glory."[14] As such, it comes as the culmination of a process of spiritual growth and seeks contemplation of God and union with Him. It is, therefore, an instrument by which God's revelation is communicated. The other way of looking at mysticism is to consider it as "life at its deepest, as a form of consciousness which includes the whole universe."[15] The feeling that fills us when we ponder the mystery surrounding our lives is also a kind of mysticism. From this point of view, we can say that there is a mystical element inherent in human nature in general.

Berdyaev emphasizes the fact that the goal of mysticism is not merely union with God, but also, and as a result of this union, a turning toward the self and toward every creature. This turning is made through love and creative activity. It is in this sense that one can say that the mission of mysticism is to free the human spirit from despondency. In the true mystical experience, the natural and the human are absorbed in the spiritual, and the gulf between the natural and the spiritual is bridged.

> True mysticism frees us from the sense of oppression which arises from everything which is alien to us . . . Mysticism means a penetration into the innermost recesses of the spiritual

[14] Berdyaev, *Freedom and the Spirit*, p. 250
[15] *Ibid.*, p. 251

world . . . here there is no separation between things and no one thing is external to another.[16]

3 THE LIGHT OF REVELATION

Revelation is the medium, the channel, through which God makes Himself known to man. Without the light of revelation man cannot find his way to freedom, he cannot be liberated from the clutch of necessity. Berdyaev is very emphatic about the direction in which revelation moves. It is a power that comes completely from without, from the world of the Spirit, from the realm of freedom. "Revelation of the divine always bears the character of a breakthrough of the other world into this world."[17] "Revelation is always an irruption through this world and not a determined historical process within it."[18]

Man's own move toward spirituality goes far, but not far enough. No matter how high the spiritual altitude he manages to reach, man can never escape the gravity of necessity. He cannot overcome the law of objectification as long as he lives within time and space, as long as he exists in the phenomenal world. There is no way for man, Berdyaev is convinced, to reach in his own ascent the height at which he would experience a condition of spiritual weightlessness. He lacks the adequate launching power. His only hope is a lift from above. When Berdyaev writes that "apart from Christianity there is no freedom,"[19] he means exactly this, since Christianity presupposes revelation. The process of symbolization through which we come to see things of the phenomenal world as symbols of another world, the realm of the spirit, is, as previously indicated, only a first step toward liberation, and it takes place in man's own consciousness. Without revelation and

[16] *Ibid.*, p. 267
[17] Berdyaev, *Truth and Revelation*, p. 54
[18] *Ibid.*, p. 144
[19] Berdyaev, *Freedom and the Spirit*, p. 121

the meanings it imparts, as we shall see later, symbolization would come to a dead end and we would be forced to take the symbol as real. The experience of mysticism, without revelation, would degenerate into a psychic experience. Man is spiritually dependent on the light of revelation, as he is physically dependent on the light of the sun.

Revelation, however, is not merely the channel but also the content channeled to us. It is not only a means of communication, but also the very supply that is communicated to us. And what is this content, this supply? For Berdyaev, it is essentially *meaning*. If symbolism tells us that the sensory world stands for some meaning, and mysticism advises us concerning the spiritual climate necessary for the attainment of meaning, revelation transmits to us that meaning. The events of the historical revelation of Christianity, the incarnation, life, death, resurrection and ascension of Christ, add up to making life *meaningful* to the believer. Through the guiding light of revelation, we discover that what seems to be a meaningless life and universe do have a definite meaning after all. To use Berdyaev's own words, "revelation is always a revelation of meaning and does not consist of outward events in themselves apart from a spiritual interpretation."[20]

But man's role as the recipient of the meaningful content of revelation is not a passive one. "Revelation is always divine-human"[21] is one of Berdyaev's frequent statements. Revelation "cannot be just one-sidedly divine. Revelation is not something which drops into man's lap from outside in which he has nothing but an entirely passive part to play."[22] In receiving revelation and interpreting

[20] Berdyaev, *Freedom and the Spirit*, p. 94
[21] Berdyaev, *Truth and Revelation*, p. 8
[22] *Ibid.*, p. 46

its content, man has always been active, though his activity has frequently been fruitless. There is nothing automatic about the manner in which he receives, interprets and assimilates what God reveals to him. Even before the waves of revelation are transmitted, a certain preparation on man's part is an essential requirement. As the rays come from above, he must prepare himself below. This preparation, explains Berdyaev, "means the permeation of man by the divine ray which brings about a change in the human mind."[23]

Berdyaev's stress on the human factor in the operations of the Spirit through revelation is unequivocal. But it is of utmost importance that we patiently and seriously follow his thinking on the paradoxical presuppositions of revelation as far as man is concerned, for this is an area which, as we shall find, will bring us closer to the meaning of his philosophy of freedom. The interaction of the divine and the human in revelation involves freedom in its divine and human aspects. To add lucidity to what he means by this "fundamental paradox of the God-manhood," Berdyaev often refers to the familiar words of Scripture "Ye shall know the truth and the truth shall make you free."[24] In *Dream and Reality*, he writes in this connection:

> Truth can make me free, and yet I can accept truth only through, and in, freedom. Thus here are two kinds of freedom, and the problem of their relation has exercised my mind in most of my writings.[25]

Revelation, through which the Truth is communicated, presupposes human freedom simply because revelation "is impossible without the fact of spiritual experience which we call faith";[26] and faith, according to Berdyaev, "is a

23 *Ibid.*, p. 54
24 John 8:32
25 Berdyaev, *Dream and Reality*, p. 47
26 Berdyaev, *Freedom and the Spirit*, p. 103

free spiritual act for without freedom faith is an impossibility."[27] "Revelation," Berdyaev writes elsewhere, "takes my freedom for granted, my act of choice, my faith in something which is still invisible and which uses no force upon me."[28]

Accordingly, there is free creativity in the very reception of revealed truth, the free consent of man himself to respond affirmatively or negatively. The activity of the whole man is involved in the process of revelation. Revelation itself is not intellectual truth, but it stimulates man's intellectual activity. Although some kind of freedom is revealed in the depth of spiritual experience,[29] yet without another kind of mysterious freedom, which man already has, that spiritual freedom cannot be transmitted through revelation. It is because of this basic fact that Berdyaev advocates a dynamic revelation and rejects any static conception of it.

> Revelation is not evolution but revolution . . . Revolution is a catastrophic transformation of consciousness, a radical modification of its structure, almost, one might say, a creation of new organs of being with functions in another world.[30]

It is in this sense that revelation brings about a spiritual awakening and a new spiritual reorientation, but, nevertheless, only with man's free consent and free cooperation.

This conception of revelation with its accent on man's creative and free participation implies certain limitations, which Berdyaev does not overlook. Inasmuch as revelation invariably seeks to reach man through himself, its content, after it has been communicated, cannot help but reflect the conditions of man and the limitations of his mind. Man's own anthropomorphism, sociomorphism, and cos-

[27] Berdyaev, *Freedom and the Spirit*, p. 107
[28] Berdyaev, *Truth and Revelation*, p. 48
[29] *Ibid.*, p. 57
[30] Berdyaev, *Freedom and the Spirit*, p. 96

momorphism leave their three-dimensional stamp on the contents of revelation.

The eternal truth of revelation must inevitably be expressed in human language with its confining molds. It must be translated into the categories of human thought with their definite boundaries and limited horizons. In order that man may understand, revelation is compelled to speak to him in the language that he knows. This is what we mean by saying that God descended to the human level, that He uses the words and idioms that are customary among the people at the time of revelation. Moreover, man can hardly refrain from reading into the truth of revelation his own human conceptions and customs. In this respect, Ludwig Feuerbach was half right in regarding religious ideas as the projection of man's own ideas. The human master-slave relation, for instance, was projected into the divine-human relationship. God became the master who is vengeful and who demands a ransom, and man became the slave who must be obedient and must sacrifice himself and his freedom for the sake of his master. There is no easy way of avoiding the imprint of necessity that the natural world and the natural man leave upon revelation. Says Berdyaev:

> The light of absolute truth is refracted as it passes through the distorting medium of human nature. The words which express the truth of revelation are all imperfect and inadequate.[31]

To project, for example, the category of causality onto God and his relation to the world is, in Berdyaev's estimation, a misapplication. Causality operates in the phenomenal world, and it is wrong to apply it to the spiritual world. "God determines nothing . . . In relation to the world God is freedom and not necessity, not determination."[32]

[31] *Ibid.*, p. 92
[32] Berdyaev, *Truth and Revelation*, p. 56

The existence of various degrees of consciousness and of spiritual maturity achieved by man, and the subsequent and corresponding degrees of "the humanization of revelation," writes Berdyaev, make us distinguish parallel and consequent stages of revelation. By the nature of the condition, revelation has to adapt itself to the level of consciousness and the degree of development that man has reached. The Old Testament revelation, for instance, was inhibited by the stage of spiritual and intellectual growth of the ancient people of Israel.

> The light of revelation spreads only in proportion to the capacity of consciousness and to the degree of receptivity which the natural man possesses for the spiritual world.[33]

This is what Jacob Boehme had in mind, Berdyaev adds, when he said that "the divine love suffers distortion through the darker elements of existence and thus appears as the divine wrath and as a consuming fire."[34] Within Christianity itself we find different degrees of revelation corresponding to the various degrees of intellectual and spiritual grasp not only in the lives of individuals but also in the history of Christianity. Every degree of revelation, says Berdyaev, is characterized by a degree of distortion corresponding to the stage of man's own consciousness and growth. Therefore, Berdyaev concludes, "what is called historical revelation upon which so much store is set is the symbolization of spiritual revelation by means of signs which belong to this phenomenal world."[35] In order to make itself intelligible, revelation must seek tangible embodiment, but in the process it gets "muffled-up in historical objectification . . . The events take place in the

[33] Berdyaev, *Freedom and the Spirit,* p. 111
[34] *Ibid.*
[35] Berdyaev, *Truth and Revelation,* p. 144

spiritual world but the image of them is formed in the world of nature and history."[36]

Nevertheless, this tragic and paradoxical fate of revelation, its distortion and objectification, which predominates wherever the church is organized after the pattern of "the kingdom of Caesar," need not be the case. In practically all periods of history, there have been men and women who were able to receive the light of revelation in its full brightness and without much distortion. There have always been the heroes of faith in whom the fire of the Spirit did not cool down, Berdyaev points out. The true mystics are striking examples, and so are the prophets, apostles, and saints.

And what is their secret? It lies in their metahistorical orientation and eschatological acclimatization. Their lives are triumphantly steered by "the new man," "the eternal man," "the transcendental man," who is active in this world, but who is of another world, the world of freedom.[37] The secret of their victorious lives and glorious freedom is hidden in the fact that while still in this world they have become citizens of the "new aeon." In order to understand what Berdyaev means by this "new aeon," which is a "triumph over the world of alienation, necessity, impersonality and hostility,"[38] we shall make an investigation of his metahistory and eschatology.

4 METAHISTORY AND ESCHATOLOGY

"Only beyond history is there victory for the spirit of God and of man."[39] Thus reads the last sentence in Berdyaev's autobiography, which was completed shortly before his death. "The solution (of the paradox of freedom and necessity) can be conceived only in forms of escha-

[36] *Ibid.*
[37] *Ibid.*, p. 18
[38] Berdyaev, *Dream and Reality*, p. 197
[39] *Ibid.*, p. 326

tology."[40] "The meaning lies beyond the confines of history."[41] These two quotations appear in Berdyaev's book, *The Beginning and the End*, published after his death, the original title of which was *Essays on Eschatological Metaphysics*.

In these few statements we can hear the theme and feel the rhythm and tempo of Berdyaev's philosophical finale. Berdyaev thought and wrote a great deal about the *Beginning* of things, but increasingly through his life, he came to view the paradox of freedom and necessity and all related problems in the light that streams from the dawn of the *End* of time and history. Early in his philosophical development, metaphysics put aside its academic gown and instead adorned itself with the existential garb of eschatology. In his introduction to *The Divine and the Human*, one of the last books he wrote, Berdyaev unequivocally describes the temper and mood of his philosophy in this manner:

> The philosophy to which I would give expression is a dramatic philosophy of destiny, of existence which is in time and passes over into eternity, of time which presses on to an end, an end which is not death but transfiguration. Everything, therefore, ought to be regarded from the point of view of the philosophy of history. And the philosophy of history can itself be nothing but prophetic, and that which unriddles the secrets of the future.[42]

All movements of Berdyaev's thought are funneled into the all-embracing and fundamental problem of the End. "The weakness of all the old systems of metaphysics," Berdyaev criticizes, "lay precisely in the fact that they were not eschatological."[43] On the other hand, his objection to

[40] Berdyaev, *The Beginning and the End*, p. 248
[41] *Ibid.*, p. 230
[42] Berdyaev, *The Divine and the Human*, p. v f
[43] Berdyaev, *The Beginning and the End*, p. 231

the types of eschatology in systems of theology is directed toward the fact that they are epistemologically and metaphysically unsound. Berdyaev proposes to remedy the malady in both traditional metaphysics and traditional theology by constructing an epistemological and metaphysical eschatology which will serve as a kind of observatory through which the past and the present with their problem of objectification and alienation may be seen in the light of the future with its new aeon of freedom and liberation.

In the towering philosophies of Kant and Hegel, for instance, the dialectic of contradictions has no solution because of the absence of a doctrine of the End of things. In his thesis, Kant proves that "the world must have a beginning and end in space and time . . . and in the 'antithesis' he proves the contradictory opposites."[44] In the antithesis, Kant finds no source of development which would eventually lead to a synthesis, as is the case with Hegel. The antinomies of Kant can be neither resolved nor overcome within the limits of the phenomenal world, and there is no End in which they will ultimately be resolved. In Hegel, despite his concept of development, there is similarly no solution. The dialectic of the finite and the infinite is continually resolved but never consummated. The synthesis immediately becomes a thesis for another dialectical development.

In Berdyaev's judgment, Kant is more correct than Hegel in saying that the antinomies cannot be resolved within the confines of our phenomenal world. But Hegel, on the other hand, was more correct than Kant in his recognition of a development through contradiction, notwithstanding his belief that the development never reaches a solution. Berdyaev gives credit to Kant and Hegel for the partial truth in their doctrines, which sheds considerable light on

[44] Wilhelm Windelband, A *History of Philosophy*, p. 550

the problem of the End of the world and of history. However, he does not hesitate to point out that the real solution is "provided only by prophetic religious experience, and that was outside the purview of both of them."[45]

It is clear that there is a paradox in thinking of the end of time, the end of history, as taking place within or outside historical time. It is hard and perhaps impossible to imagine the End as an event belonging either to this world or to the next. In order to clarify the issue, Berdyaev makes use of his three categories of time—cosmic, historical, and existential time, which were discussed in the last part of the third chapter. Cosmic time, which is cyclical in its movement, governs nature. Historical time, symbolized by the straight line, constitutes the stage of the human drama. Existential time, illustrated by the point, is the trickling of eternity into historical time.

The End is the conquest of both cosmic and historical time. It is not an end in time but of time. This End occurs in existential time, which is the only time that remains. But since existential time is anchored in eternity, this is equivalent to saying that the End takes place in eternity. However, for Berdyaev, eternity is not a distant reality. Drops from the ocean of eternity keep falling into our historical time. These are the moments of existential time which constantly seek to penetrate and permeate our historical time and existence. A person experiencing such a moment would not watch the clock and calendar.

All acts of creativity, explains Berdyaev, are performed in existential time when man forgets the flow of cosmic and historical time. This "break-through" of eternity into this world of cosmic and historical time is what Berdyaev calls "Metahistory."[46] We can be elevated to such *metahistorical* moments only through a religious experience.

[45] Berdyaev, *The Divine and the Human*, p. 196
[46] Berdyaev, *The Beginning and the End*, p. 166

"The end is a spiritual event which takes place in existential time."[47]

Every experience of existential time, every metahistorical experience, is an experience of the End of historical and cosmic time. Through such an experience, meaning is transmitted. "The End is the triumph of meaning."[48]

Only from the viewpoint of the End does the history of the world and mankind have meaning. A history without an End would be meaningless. An endless march of time, Berdyaev thinks, would mean the triumph of death. The End is identical with the goal. History has meaning if it is consummated in such a goal. Personal and historical existence can have meaning only as they are seen in the long-range perspective of their ultimate goal.

From the philosophical point of view, the End of history and of the world is the victory of freedom over necessity, of spiritualization over objectification. In this present aeon, inconspicuous metahistorical forces, armed with *meaning*, infiltrate through acts of creativeness into the world of phenomena, and prepare the work of ultimate triumph of spirit over nature, of freedom over necessity. "The metahistorical arrives out of the world of the noumenal into this objective world and revolutionizes it."[49]

Berdyaev speaks of this metahistorical revolution within historical time not only as the End of what has been, but also as the Beginning of what is to be, namely, "the new aeon," "the new spirituality." This is what he means when he says that "history is pregnant with newness which enters into the eschatology of history and is an influence which exerts a pull towards an end by which everything is resolved."[50]

[47] *Ibid.*, p. 252
[48] Berdyaev, *The Divine and the Human*, p. 197
[49] Berdyaev, *The Beginning and the End*, p. 211 f
[50] *Ibid.*, p. 166

But the conception of this newness is effected by the noumenal world, the world of the spirit and freedom. The newness and the new aeon have been initiated by what Berdyaev calls "the metahistorical event par excellence,"[51] that is, the appearance of Jesus Christ.

> The appearance of Christ the Liberator is a metahistorical fact and it occurred in existential time. But in that central messianic manifestation meta-history breaks through history, albeit history receives it in a troubled setting.[52]

The new spirituality that Christ injects into this world implies a transition from spiritual symbolism to spiritual realization. It means a victory of subjectivity over objectivity. But the new spirituality with its complete victory of freedom over necessity, made possible through the intervention of metahistory in the progression of history, is fully realized only in the hinterland of eschatology. "My faith in victory is eschatological."[53]

The eschatological element in Berdyaev's thinking is very dominant. Everything must pass through the ultimate refinery of eschatology in order to be freed from the impure particles of necessity. "Metaphysics inevitably become an eschatology."[54] "A transition to eschatological Christianity is inevitable."[55]

Christianity is not merely historical but also eschatological; and eschatological Christianity is messianic Christianity. In Christian eschatology God's self-revelation reaches its completeness. But the road to this culmination from the human side is not easy. It involves a stern struggle and demands sacrifice and suffering. The final stage of this

[51] Berdyaev, *The Beginning and the End*, p. 167
[52] *Ibid.*, p. 211
[53] *Ibid.*, p. 253
[54] *Ibid.*, p. 231
[55] *Ibid.*, p. 212

road is painted by Berdyaev with the dark apocalyptic gray of *godlessness* and *godforsakenness.*

Berdyaev's eschatology, however, is not fatalistic apocalypticism. Our attitude toward the End of this world and the beginning of the new world, Berdyaev stresses, should not be passive. Often in the history of Christianity, apocalyptic expectations have led to a passive waiting for the End, and a foolish reluctance to face the issues of the day. Eschatology does not imply such an escape. "It is a call to transfigure this evil and stricken world."[56]

Berdyaev proclaims an active and dynamic eschatology. Our waiting for the End must be positive and creative. In fact every creative act of man is eschatological in character, and is a metahistorical moment in which the world of phenomena comes to an end. The end of the world is brought about by divine-human activity. Man's creative work is an important factor in the preparation for, and culmination of, the End. This is so because the End is not merely a negative event of judgment and destruction but one of illumination and transfiguration. The End is the result of a positive process of transformation which is already taking place in this world through the creative activity of man. "The creative act of man is needed for the coming of the Kingdom of God, God is in need of and awaits it."[57] Berdyaev's eschatological outlook "embraces in its view every moment of life. At each moment of one's living, what is needed is to put an end to the old world and to begin the new."[58]

Active eschatology means, therefore, a transformation of the world here and now. The world is transformed by transforming the people in it. From being merely human, men should become divine-human. As a matter of fact,

[56] Berdyaev, *Dream and Reality*, p. 291
[57] Berdyaev, *The Beginning and the End*, p. 251 f
[58] *Ibid.*, p. 254

men are not human unless they are divine-human. The specific qualities of the new man who has been transformed have been revealed in Jesus Christ, the God-man. He restored the communion between God and alienated man. Man's fall, his original sin, says Berdyaev, was not so much an act of disobedience as an act of self-assertion which resulted in self-isolation and the loss of the true image of God. Fallen man, ceasing to be divine-human, degenerated to the human level and frequently disintegrates into an inhuman and unhuman animal. Alienation from God always leads to alienation from self and from one's fellow men.

The mysterious work of redemption through Christ is the process by which fallen man is restored by inner transformation. Berdyaev's theology here is strictly Pauline.[59] The true Christian is the person who has experienced this spiritual transformation and who is creatively active in transforming society by helping others have the same experience. The new man, the transcendental man, who has been freed from slavery to the objectified world now devotes his creative energies to transfiguring the world, to the building of God's Kingdom, and thus contributes toward bringing about the consummation of the new aeon.

In the chapter "Christianity and History" in *The Meaning of History*, Berdyaev discusses the liberation of the new man by Christ "in the fullness of time" when there was genuine longing for redemption and when both Greek philosophy and Judaism could no longer satisfy the spiritual needs of men. "The essential contribution of Christianity therefore lay in that it liberated man and offered a free solution for human destiny."[60] Christianity inaugurated the new era, the new aeon, of which the true Christian is an active citizen. The regenerated Christian plays

[59] As expounded especially in Romans 1–11
[60] Berdyaev, *The Meaning of History*, p. 114

an important role through his creative activity in consummating the End and initiating the perfect reign of existential communion between man and God and man and his fellow men. Every single creative act puts an end to the rule of necessity and confirms that domain "where God's power is revealed in freedom and in love."[61]

Berdyaev stresses the point that morality constitutes a major part of the creativity of the new man. In fact, for him, eschatological morality is the only true morality. Every moral act of love, compassion, sacrifice, ends the rule of necessity and begins the rule of freedom. The person who performs a moral act brings about the end of this world; he leaves behind him this world and enters into the other world, the world of the new spirituality, the aeon of the Holy Spirit.

The transformed life of the Christian possesses eternity during its earthly existence. Its destiny is not changed by physical death. Immortality has been won in this life by the struggle of the personality. The full realization of the eternal life, however, is reached at and through the resurrection when the whole body-soul-spirit entity is transformed into an incorruptible spiritual body. This means the self-fulfillment of the human personality, the highest value not only in time but also in eternity. Despite the inescapable struggle of the personality in this life, which is imperative for its attainment of immortality, this attainment itself is an act of God's grace. "Grace must be the power which is called upon to resolve the contradiction between freedom and necessity."[62]

A final word about Berdyaev's eschatology that must be said is that it is universal in its outlook. Berdyaev is indignant about the pessimistic eschatology that conceives of eternal torments in hell as the triumph of divine justice.

[61] Berdyaev, *Dream and Reality*, p. 298
[62] Berdyaev, *The Beginning and the End*, p. 247

Even Christianity is not free from this "vengeful and cruel eschatology." The idea of justice can so easily assume the function of retaliation. It is also wrong to suppose that the doctrine of eternal torment serves to frighten people into salvation. The end never justifies the means. The experience of hell is the experience of godlessness, which belongs to this life and not to the next. Berdyaev also abhors an optimistic eschatology, which projects into heaven an earthly kingdom of the senses or forms an estimate of eternity in terms of time. It is distastefully wrong to ascribe to heaven sensual qualities that are characteristic of the present life, and it is horribly ugly to think of the justified in paradise finding delight in contemplating the pains of sinners in hell. "Eschatology must be free from pessimism and from optimism born of rationalization. All rationalistic eschatologies are a horrible nightmare."[63]

Berdyaev's eschatology emphasizes the inevitability of a universal salvation. Salvation cannot be limited to a chosen people or to certain individuals. There is salvation either for all or for none; and Berdyaev casts his vote with the former. "One cannot be saved in loneliness and isolation. Salvation can only be a corporate experience, a universal release from suffering."[64] Pain, tragedy, and misfortune will go on and on in this world until all mankind and the whole world are saved, transfigured, and regenerated.[65]

The Christian hope is universal in character. It looks forward, says Berdyaev, to "a general resurrection and transfiguration."[66] The doctrine of "a retaliatory and penal eschatology" in Christianity is an indication that a universal consciousness has not yet been fully realized and that the spirit of love has not yet replaced the spirit of the law. The great temptation of eschatology is to return

[63] Berdyaev, *The Destiny of Man*, p. 282
[64] Berdyaev, *The Beginning and the End*, p. 237
[65] Berdyaev, *The Destiny of Man*, p. 294
[66] Berdyaev, *The Beginning and the End*, p. 238

to the categories of time and thus expose itself to the process of objectification. We must not transfer to the province of eschatology the characteristics of the world of phenomena. In other words, we must not objectify the End by projecting into it our passionate dream of paradise or our wild emotions of vengeance. Neither should we stifle the Christian idea of God by the categories of our sociomorphism, anthropomorphism, and cosmomorphism with all their implications. God is not like anything at all in this world of objectification.

God is that victory of light over darkness which is being achieved in eternity, the triumph of meaning over senselessness, of beauty over ugliness, of freedom over necessity.[67]

[67] *Ibid.*, p. 253

CHAPTER VII

A PHILOSOPHY OF FREEDOM

1 IN RETROSPECT

Earlier in the course of this study, the major influences to which Berdyaev was exposed were surveyed. His personal sharing in the history and destiny of the Russian people lent an existential flavor to his philosophy of freedom. Berdyaev's thinking reflects his own longing for freedom.

Berdyaev acknowledges his debt to a host of intellectual ancestors. Khomyakov sowed in his heart and mind the seeds of reverence for the free creative spirit. Herzen showed him the close link between freedom and personality. Pushkin gave a patriotic bent to his love for freedom. Belinsky enlisted his talents for the continued fight against Hegel in the name of personality. Tolstoy intensified his awareness of the manifold forms of slavery in civilization. Dostoyevsky guided him into the mystifying gallery of freedom and showed him its contradictions and peculiarities. Solovyev's penetrating analysis of ·freedom and his contention that necessity does not exclude freedom, as well as his universal outlook, gave added depth to Berdyaev's thinking on freedom. Boehme answered Berdyaev's ontological search with his doctrine of the *Ungrund*, which Berdyaev identified with primordial freedom. The Kantian thesis that man's liberation from the necessity of nature is realized by his obedience to the metaphysical law within his own will injected into Berdyaev's theory of freedom an ethical subjectivism. Kierkegaard, on the other hand, through his dictum "Truth is subjectivity," provided him with an effective existential weapon with which to fight Hegelianism.

The inquiry into Berdyaev's philosophical anthropology revealed that his conception of man follows the dualistic tradition. Man is a meeting place of two worlds; he is both divine and human. It was then shown that the fundamental paradox of freedom and necessity is the product of Berdyaev's dualistic anthropological philosophy. This paradox operates in nature, society, civilization, and history. As a natural being, man finds himself under the rule of natural necessity. As a social being, he must be a part of society, which often coerces him by its conventions. With the progress of civilization, the very world which man creates to liberate himself from the tyranny of nature, he increasingly becomes the servant of what he creates. And as a historical being, man finds himself under the grip of historical necessity.

The effects of the paradox of freedom and necessity on the human personality were then analyzed. Through the process of objectification, man's personality, which Berdyaev conceives as an ethical and spiritual entity, is used as a means to various ends. This alienation expresses itself in depersonalization and dehumanization. Man's worth is then measured by what he possesses and not by what he is. Thus the human personality and, with it, freedom is destroyed.

The possibility of a solution to the paradox of freedom and necessity in Berdyaev's philosophy was then investigated. The concept of creativity was discovered to be the key to the solution. In its strictest ontological sense, creativity is bringing something out of nothing. For Berdyaev, this is equivalent to creating out of freedom, the absence of determination. The divine image in man implies the capacity and the duty to engage in creative work. It was observed how Berdyaev makes a distinction between the creative activity itself, which is liberating, and the created product, which becomes part of the objectified world of necessity.

The "ethics of creativeness," according to Berdyaev, is the highest form of ethics, and is engaged in the creation of values. Through creativity, man frees himself from the chains of necessity. Artistic creativity, for instance, is a liberating activity. By seeking the truth about everything, philosophy releases man from the prison of necessity. Berdyaev insists that philosophy must be conceived as an art and not as a science.

The final solution of the paradox of freedom and necessity, in Berdyaev's view, is spiritual. To interpret the natural world symbolically, that is, to see physical phenomena as signs of spiritual realities, is the first step toward the solution. The principle of objectification is counteracted by the process of symbolization. Another significant step in that direction is made through mysticism, which is the spiritual uplift that makes possible the intuitive perception of spiritual realities. The union with God achieved through mysticism is a powerhouse that generates love and creative activity. It frees man from the world of necessity. Within the mystical experience, man is given the light of revelation to guide him to freedom. If the symbol points to the meaning of things, revelation communicates that meaning. Christianity has the revealed truth which makes life meaningful. The liberating truth cannot be imposed on man. It can be received by him only freely.

In Berdyaev's view, the solution of the paradox of freedom and necessity cannot be fully realized in this present life. The conflict between freedom and necessity continues throughout man's earthly existence. However, he can experience the breakthrough of eternity into historical time. Through such metahistorical experiences, as Berdyaev designates them, man gains insight into the meaning that lies

behind the phenomenal world. Understanding the meaning of things and events is experienced as victory of freedom over necessity, a triumph of spiritualization over
objectification.

The coming of Jesus Christ marked the beginning of
the new aeon whose consummation lies beyond the confines of history. Man is called upon to contribute through
his creative activity to bring about the transformation and
transfiguration of the world. He is enabled to do this by
being redeemed and restored to what he was before the
Fall, a divine-human being. Whoever undergoes this fundamental spiritual change is a *new man*, a *transcendental
man*, who has been liberated from the sway of necessity.
A *new man* is able to dedicate himself to creative activity
by which the world is transfigured. Morality constitutes a
major part of this creativity. To practice love, compassion,
and sacrifice is to help bring about the victory of freedom
over necessity.

2   A DYNAMIC DEVELOPMENT

Before we attempt to draw conclusions about the nature
of Berdyaev's philosophy, more light needs to be shed on
his concept of freedom. We shall try to do this by seeing
this fundamental concept in the perspective of Berdyaev's
entire intellectual life and spiritual development. Misunderstanding and misinterpretation will result if the
process of growth and maturation is overlooked. Berdyaev
went through several stages in his philosophical development. To stop at one particular stage and to evaluate his
work at that point, a temptation to which some of his
critics have yielded, will lead to a misrepresentation of the
facts.

Berdyaev himself was keenly aware of the process of
development his thinking had undergone, and attempted
to trace its course in his autobiography. He refers, for instance, to two of his books, *Philosophy of Freedom* (1911)

and *Freedom and the Spirit* (1926), "which express my approach to this problem (of freedom) at different stages in the development of my philosophy."[1] At one juncture early in his life, Marx and Nietzsche were competing for his attention and loyalty. At another period, Berdyaev tells us, "the Nietzschean element had the upper hand, but in the end it was the Tolstoyan that prevailed."[2]

The philosophical road which Berdyaev traveled had three main stages. The first is materialistic Marxism. It was preceded by revolutionary, liberal tendencies, and was followed by a transitional period of mystical anarchism. The second major station at which Berdyaev tarried for a while is metaphysical idealism. This began with a short aesthetic and romantic prelude. The third stage is Christian existentialism. Speculation gave way to mysticism. The prophetic and ethical elements came to be the dominant ones in Berdyaev's thinking. Most vital for the understanding of his concept of freedom is recognition of the fact that his "thought moved increasingly toward the problems of ethics," as he informs us in *Dream and Reality*. "The idea of what 'ought to be,'" Berdyaev goes on to say, "came to predominate over the idea of what 'is.'"[3] This movement from ontology to ethics in his life and thinking has often been overlooked or ignored by some of his critics. The result is a misunderstanding of what he meant, for example, by *uncreated freedom*.

The existential quality of Berdyaev's thinking and writing must be borne in mind if the meaning of his concept of freedom, the backbone of his philosophy, is to be clearly comprehended. Berdyaev never wrote just for the sake of philosophizing but in order to give expression to his own experience. What he wrote was part of his total reaction to interior and exterior environment.

[1] Berdyaev, *Dream and Reality*, p. 52
[2] *Ibid.*, p. 63
[3] *Ibid.*, p. 87

All the tensions and contradictions in life are, and ought to be, reflected in one's philosophy, and one should not attempt to compose them for the sake of neat philosophical construction. Philosophy cannot ever be divorced from the totality of man's spiritual experience, from his struggles, his insights, his ecstasies, his religious faith and mystical vision.[4]

My philosophy is a philosophy of existence, . . . that is to say, it gives expression to the problems and wrestlings of man: it is, in this sense, very close indeed to life.[5]

Berdyaev's thought and life must be taken as a whole. The gradual and abrupt changes in his historical existence were echoed in his thinking. It is vitally important to read his earlier works in the light of his later writings and with due sensitiveness to the circumstances and crises that prevailed at the time he wrote. As Donald A. Lowrie reminds us, in order to assess the apparent contradictions in Berdyaev's philosophy, "it must be recalled that Berdyaev's books cover nearly half a century of his developing thought —and what a stormy development it was!"[6] Whenever Berdyaev wrote, he was responding to the entire historical milieu and often to some personal crisis as well. "I write in response to an inner voice which commands me to transmit my mental experience. Writing is no luxury for me but a means of survival, an almost physiological necessity."[7]

When Berdyaev moved from one stage to another in his development, he took along as a part of his philosophical cargo his altered thoughts about old ideas, the original forms of which he found necessary to discard. Although he did change his philosophical route, as mentioned above, he did not always and entirely give up his ideological guideposts. Reviewing his evolvement in his autobiog-

[4] Berdyaev, *Dream and Reality*, p. 104

[5] *Ibid.*, p. 24

[6] Donald Lowrie, *Rebellious Prophet: A Life of Nicolas Berdyaev*, p. 244

[7] Berdyaev, *Dream and Reality*, p. 220

raphy, he tells us that from time to time during his intellectual development he acquired new philosophic insight and expressions, but that his "work as a whole revolved round a single axis and has a number of constant dominant themes which give it an inward unity, however fragmentary and aphoristic its outward form may be."[8]

The single axis around which Berdyaev's life and thought revolved, it was shown in the previous chapters, was freedom in its paradoxical relation to necessity. "The problem of freedom . . . is at the centre of all my writings."[9] Berdyaev refers to *The Philosophy of Freedom* (1911) as his "first book on freedom," but as he looks back over the span of thirty-five years to evaluate this work he frankly writes: "I must confess that this book does not satisfy me at all any more."[10] In this "first book on freedom" he addressed himself to the problem of theodicy and adopted Boehme's concept of the *Ungrund*, which he identified with "uncreated or uncaused freedom," in order to free God from the responsibility for evil and suffering. But this "first attempt" at reaching a solution he later on regarded "as an unfinished outline of the matter in question,"[11] and as "unsatisfactory because I was still beset by the associations of the Idealist ontology and used the terminology characteristic of this philosophy."[12]

Evidence of a dynamic development in Berdyaev's thinking, and his awareness of it, may also be derived from his own assessment of his next important book, *The Meaning of the Creative Act* (1916). This work marked the aesthetic and romantic period of his development and was sown with philosophical ideas which blossomed and reached fruition in later works. It was in this volume that

8 *Ibid.*, p. 285
9 *Ibid.*, p. 100
10 *Ibid.*
11 *Ibid.*, p. 179
12 *Ibid.*, p. 212

he struck the fundamental note of creative freedom which became the *leitmotif* of his philosophical thought. Nevertheless, the views expressed in that book should not be taken as final. It was written under much intellectual strain and excitement, Berdyaev informs us in his autobiography,[13] and was also composed about the time he went to Italy, which made a powerful impression on him. "I felt completely carried away."[14] No wonder he describes this book, despite its importance, "as an impulsive, unpremeditated and unfinished work."[15]

To state and analyze Berdyaev's meaning of freedom, therefore, it is necessary to use a dynamic approach, remembering his own advice that "freedom must be looked at dialectically and in movement."[16] An important guideline is the process of intellectual and spiritual development in Berdyaev himself, in which, as he says, "the search for meaning preceded in me the search for God, and the search for the eternal was prior to the search for redemption."[17] The fact must be kept in view that in Berdyaev's thought there was a movement from ontology to ethics and that increasingly "the will ruled the intellect and the philosophic imagination."[18]

3   AN EXISTENTIAL DIALECTIC OF FREEDOM

The designation "Existential Dialectic" is taken from Berdyaev's last writings. The Russian title of *The Divine and the Human* is *Existential Dialectic of the Divine and the Human* (1947). The expression *existential dialectic of freedom* appears in *The Beginning and the End*[19]

[13] Berdyaev, *Dream and Reality*, p. 100
[14] *Ibid.*, p. 211
[15] *Ibid.*, p. 210
[16] Berdyaev, *Truth and Revelation*, p. 71
[17] Berdyaev, *Dream and Reality*, p. 14
[18] *Ibid.*, p. 87
[19] Berdyaev, *The Beginning and the End*, p. 105

(1952), which was published in Russian under the title *An Essay in Eschatological Metaphysics* (1947). The same expression is also found in *The Realm of Spirit and the Realm of Caesar*[20] (1949). In this same work, Berdyaev stresses the fact that "the static idea of freedom is not valid" and that "against this we must assert the dynamic conception of freedom, freedom as creative movement."[21]

Again, in his very last volume, *Truth and Revelation* (1954), he insists that "the creative philosophy of freedom . . . is not ontological but existential."[22] Berdyaev's dialectic of freedom is not theoretical in the Hegelian sense. It is, rather, existential because it is grounded in, and arises out of, his own personal life and experience. This existential quality of Berdyaev's philosophy of freedom became apparent in the course of our study of the dynamic development of his thought. Once the movement from ontology to ethics in Berdyaev's philosophical evolution is recognized it becomes possible to unravel the dialectic of his freedom. The numerous descriptions of freedom representing various shades of meaning that we find in his books, such as original, primeval, uncreated, pre-cosmic, primary, meonic, fathomless, pre-existent, initial, underived, indeterminate, irrational, rational, human, potential, creative, spiritual, personal, final, gained, gratuitous, existential and a few others—indeed a bewildering jungle of references—can then be reduced to three distinct categories, namely, the freedom of self-determination, the freedom of self-perfection and the freedom of self-realization.[23]

[20] Berdyaev, *The Realm of Spirit and the Realm of Caesar*, p. 104

[21] *Ibid.*, p. 111

[22] Berdyaev, *Truth and Revelation*, p. 74 f

[23] A somewhat similar classification has been used by Mortimer J. Adler (ed.), *The Idea of Freedom* (New York: Doubleday & Co., 2 volumes, 1958, 1961) in which all types of freedom

Berdyaev experienced freedom and thought of it, first of all, in terms of self-determination. Freedom as self-determination is variously described by him as initial, primordial, original, unfathomable, irrational and uncreated. Expressed negatively, this type of freedom is simply the absence of all determination outside man himself. Positively, freedom as self-determination is the kind of freedom with which everyone is born. When Berdyaev says, "Freedom brought me to Christ,"[24] he means freedom as self-determination. He was not coerced in his coming to Christ by anything or anybody. Freedom as self-determination is what Berdyaev has in mind when he writes, "I come of my own freedom to know the truth which (in its turn) liberates me."[25] He is more specific about this initial freedom when he states that

> freedom is my own norm and my own creation of good and evil . . . freedom is first and foremost my independence, determination from within and creative initiative.[26]

Freedom as self-determination constitutes the thesis of Berdyaev's existential dialectic. Freedom as the thesis must be understood as it operated on two levels of his own life. Freedom as self-determination is the kind of freedom that preoccupied him in the earlier stages of his intellectual development. It is also the type of freedom with which he made his response to life throughout his life. The freedom of self-determination was a quality, a condition, of Berdyaev's entire life; but it ceased to be the chief object of

---

throughout the history of philosophy are reduced to three: "Natural freedom of self-determination," "Acquired freedom of self-perfection," and "Circumstantial freedom of self-realization." With a few exceptions, Berdyaev does not figure in this voluminous work.

[24] Berdyaev, *Freedom and the Spirit*, p. x
[25] Berdyaev, *Dream and Reality*, p. 53
[26] *Ibid.*, p. 52

his speculation a few years after his permanent exile from Russia.

In his earlier writings, Berdyaev often referred to this original freedom as *uncreated freedom*. Obviously, this terminology carried an ontological connotation and implication. Apparently, uncreated freedom provided the metaphysical answer to Berdyaev's ontological inquiry during the time when he could not accept the traditional Christian view with regard to the origin of evil, and before he could develop a view of his own. He had adopted Boehme's doctrine of the *Ungrund*, that dark abyss, which is pure, aimless, empty, and undetermined will, although he rejected Boehme's contention that the *Ungrund* is located in the Godhead and insisted that it is outside the Godhead. The *Ungrund*, which Berdyaev interpreted to mean the primal freedom, has its origin in the *meonic stuff*. This stuff, according to Berdyaev, is indeterminate Nothing, indeterminate freedom, which is uncreated. This preexistent freedom is potentially the source of good and evil. The differentiation between good and evil was brought about by God's creative act. The fact that evil and suffering have their origin in uncreated freedom, in Berdyaev's judgment, may have absolved God from being responsible for their existence.

Moreover, when God created the world and man, He used the pre-existent meonic stuff which potentially contained uncreated freedom. Uncreated freedom, which carried the seeds of man's freedom of self-determination, therefore, went into the making of man. God created him in His divine image, that is, made him a created creator endowed with spiritual freedom. Prior to his falling away from God, man lived in a state of innocence because his human freedom of self-determination, which had its origin in uncreated freedom, had not unfolded itself as yet.[27]

[27] Berdyaev, *The Destiny of Man*, p. 36

The "fall" came when man's initial freedom of self-determination expressed itself and he "began to make distinctions and evaluations, tasted the fruit of the tree of knowledge and found himself on this side of good and evil."[28] By falling away from God, man loses the divine image and, with it, his spiritual freedom. He is no longer a created creator but merely a creature. But Berdyaev does not think man loses his human freedom of self-determination through the "fall." On the contrary, he retains the freedom which was the cause of his first "fall," and it continues to be the cause of his repeated falls in this earthly life.

Freedom as self-determination is irrational and often leads man into a state of slavery. Through it, man separates himself from the divine center. Man's own self-determination carries within itself no guarantee that the right path will be followed. Berdyaev continues to argue convincingly that man, by his own choice, by his own self-determination, frequently takes the path of discord and hatred and thus generates evil and suffering. Quite often, our own freedom of self-determination locks us up in the prison of necessity. Berdyaev explains the irrational character of this first freedom by saying that "initial freedom has not been sanctified in love, it has not been illuminated by the inner light of truth."[29] Therefore, freedom as self-determination by itself is inadequate. It may give rise to both good and evil. History testifies that it has been the cause of much more evil and suffering than of good and happiness. Man's freedom of self-determination itself needs to be liberated from its own self-centeredness. Man needs another kind of freedom, which comes to him from another source. What is that second type of freedom, according to Berdyaev?

[28] Berdyaev, *The Destiny of Man*, p. 36
[29] Berdyaev, *Freedom and the Spirit*, p. 132

Berdyaev describes this other freedom as rational, intelligent, and final. It comes to us, or rather, is acquired by us, "through reason, truth and goodness."[30] Man has freedom as self-determination at the moment of his birth, but he has to struggle throughout his life to realize this second freedom, freedom as self-perfection. The Greeks in general recognized only this type of freedom, which is the gift of truth but which is acquired through knowledge of the truth. To attain it means to be controlled by the highest spiritual principles. Freedom as self-perfection is offered to man through the moral law. He acquires it through his submission to this law.

Berdyaev believes that freedom as self-perfection is never completely and permanently actualized in man's historical existence because submission to the moral law, the means by which it is acquired, leads to compulsory virtue and, with it, to slavery. In our present existence, there is only partial and occasional assimilation of truth. The assimilation must be whole and continuous if freedom as self-perfection is to be realized. Moreover, this second freedom is threatened by the danger of degenerating into its opposite, which happens whenever the truth becomes institutionalized and controlled by some authority. Whenever man is compelled to obey the moral law, and the truth is imposed upon him by force, usually in the name of peace, happiness, and security and with the promise of being freed from the burden of choice, his moral life becomes mechanized. This means man's freedom of self-determination is suppressed, and his freedom of self-perfection is distorted. Therein lies the tragedy: the rational freedom of self-perfection, working through organized institutions, reduces life into a "series of arbitrary and mechanical relationships" and creates a "necessitarian freedom in and through necessity."[31]

30 *Ibid.*, p. 125
31 *Ibid.*, p. 134

Berdyaev cites the New Testament words "Ye shall know the truth and the truth shall make you free" as containing a conditional promise of this rational freedom. However, these words, he says, have been rephrased by all sorts of philosophies and applied to propagate various kinds of alleged truths. To Marxism, for instance, knowledge of the truth is equivalent to knowledge of necessity and, consequently, freedom is knowledge of necessity. In true Christianity, the truth does not come to us as a moral law, but as a Person who is the Way and the Life and who does not violate or ignore man's freedom of self-determination. The Truth of Christianity respects man's personality, recognizes its value, and makes His appeal through man's own freedom of self-determination. But before we go into this, we must first contrast the freedom of self-determination and the freedom of self-perfection, the thesis and the antithesis of Berdyaev's existential dialectic, and see the paradoxical nature of their relationship.

Berdyaev thinks that these two freedoms need not and should not exclude each other. Unfortunately, instead of supplementing each other, they often contradict each other. Now the one, then the other, seems to have its way. In either case, the result is the loss of freedom. In the words of Berdyaev,

> If the first kind of freedom spells anarchy which ends by annihilating liberty, the second gives rise to an arbitrary organization of life, whether theocratic or communistic, in which the freedom of the spirit and of conscience is entirely destroyed.[32]

> The first kind of liberty means division and disunion. The second strives to subject this division and disunion to the control of organized truth and goodness.[33]

[32] Berdyaev, *Freedom and the Spirit*, p. 133
[33] *Ibid.*, p. 134

Thus instead of being liberated from the grip of necessity, man finds himself more ruthlessly enslaved. The question is how to bring harmony into chaos, how to reconcile the two freedoms, the freedom of self-determination and the freedom of self-perfection, how to bring peace where there is war.

According to Berdyaev, the thesis and the antithesis are resolved in a synthesis, a third kind of freedom which serves as a differential mechanism in balancing the irrational and rational freedoms, an agent well-qualified to reconcile the two. In *Freedom and the Spirit*, Berdyaev writes, "there is revealed to us a third kind of liberty which is a reconciliation of the two other kinds."[34]

Freedom as self-realization is Berdyaev's answer to the contradictions of the first two freedoms. He establishes this synthesis of his existential dialectic of freedom on a strong theological foundation. Only through self-realization and self-fulfillment can man achieve true freedom. This is possible through the religion of the God-man, the great Liberator, Jesus Christ, Berdyaev declares. In Him there is a union of the two natures of God and man. Christ is both God and man in the absolute sense. This means that both man's freedom of self-determination and the freedom of self-perfection which has its source in the divine, but consists in obedience to the moral law, are combined in the Person of Christ. The grace of Christ brings harmony between them. The Truth, which is the Living Lord, does not constrain us. Through grace, the Redeemer acts from within our freedom of self-determination. He illuminates its irrationality. The grace of Christ also operates on the freedom of self-perfection by restraining the coerciveness of the moral law. The point must be stressed, says Berdyaev, that the source of true freedom is in God, not as Father but as the Son who is the God-man.

[34] *Ibid.*, p. 135

To receive the freedom of Christ is not only to receive the freedom of God but to receive also, by partaking of Christ's human nature, that freedom which enables man to turn to God.[35]

Because Christ is not only God but also man in the absolute sense, man's freedom of self-determination has participated in the work of redemption. Berdyaev stresses the human factor to the point of including the whole of mankind as active participants through the humanity of Christ in the work of salvation. "In the grace which comes from the Son not only divine but also human energy is at work."[36] Berdyaev's emphasis on the human component of the freedom that Christ brings is unmistakable:

Here we see the third kind of freedom, namely, that of man, in an active and illuminated state. It is, in fact, freedom united to grace and love, and sanctified by grace.[37]

But he places equal stress on the new force that enters the picture and works within man, eliminating the evil potentialities of his freedom of self-determination and illuminating its irrational tendencies. This illumination is a victory over necessity. The manner in which this is brought about, the means by which it is accomplished, are of utmost importance. The crucified Christ does not force anyone to recognize Him as the Son of God, as the Liberator of mankind. His divine power is expressed in the silent activity of faith and love. The crucified Truth is void of all logical and judicial power. There is nothing compulsory about its appeal to men. It does not impose itself upon man. It presupposes, and addresses itself to, man's freedom of self-determination. Redemption frees human liberty from evil not by means of coercion but by grace,

[35] Berdyaev, *Freedom and the Spirit*, p. 137
[36] *Ibid.*, p. 139
[37] *Ibid.*

which works from within man's freedom of self-determination itself. That is why Berdyaev identifies the Christian doctrine of grace with true freedom.[38]

Berdyaev must be closely followed here into the mystical chambers of his intuition if what he means by this third variety of freedom is to be clearly understood. The freedom of Christ, according to Berdyaev, is absolute spiritual freedom. However, inasmuch as all mankind participates in the humanity of Christ, all men find in Him the inner source of their freedom.[39] In the same context Berdyaev says that in and through Christ the whole of mankind makes its free response to God. We participate in Christ's work of redemption through an inner mystical communion with Him.[40] "We triumph over evil only in communion with Christ and in cooperation with His work, through the bearing of His Cross."[41]

Berdyaev considers death an evil imposed upon man by the lower and external world to which he is subjected through sin. However, by following the example of Christ, who knew no sin and yet freely accepted Calvary and death, as well as by accepting death as the inevitable consequence of sin, redeemed man is able to overcome it spiritually. The way which leads to

> transfiguration of the world into eternal life . . . involves the free acceptance of the cross, suffering and death . . . The light which shines from the Crucified is a light shining in the darkness.[42]

Man attains the "freedom of Christ" through faithful communion with Him and by following in His steps. They lead to agony before they lead to glory, but it is only

[38] *Ibid.*, p. 135
[39] *Ibid.*, p. 137
[40] *Ibid.*, p. 180
[41] *Ibid.*, p. 187
[42] *Ibid.*, p. 188

through this "Christian freedom" that man finds self-realization and self-fulfillment.

At times, Berdyaev refers to this synthesis, that is, freedom of self-realization, as existential freedom. This is so because the *freedom of Christ* involves the very depth of his existence. As such, it consists of "two processes, seemingly incompatible but by the paradox of life, really complementary, one redemptive, the other creative."[43]

So far, only the redemptive aspect of this third freedom has been discussed. For Berdyaev, this aspect is essentially an inner "liberation from something" such as guilt, fear of life and death. There is another aspect to this freedom which is "liberation for the sake of something." "And this 'for the sake of,'" explains Berdyaev, "is creativeness."[44]

For Berdyaev, "Creative freedom" is this creative function of "the freedom of Christ," which is the freedom of self-realization. Redeemed man as a transformed and transfigured person possesses this creative freedom, by which he creates a new and better world. Creativeness is always a movement from the world to God. Its products are in time, but its creative activity partakes of eternity. Creativeness is victory over necessity, determination and time. The fact must be emphasized that creative freedom, in Berdyaev's view, is fundamentally ethical in nature. It is in this sense that "creativeness is the way of liberation."[45] In relation to other people, creative freedom always has a moral content. It is "an act of love, of pity, of help, of peace-making."[46]

The highest form of ethics, according to Berdyaev, is the "ethics of creativeness." And the objective of this ethics is spiritual: "Inner conquest of slavery is the fundamental task of moral life."[47] Berdyaev bases his entire ethics on

[43] Berdyaev, *Dream and Reality*, p. 210
[44] Berdyaev, *The Destiny of Man*, p. 147
[45] *Ibid.*, p. 147
[46] *Ibid.*, p. 148
[47] *Ibid.*, p. 147

this creative freedom released in redeemed man by Christ's redemptive work.

The creative freedom of the liberated man operates through two channels: struggle and contemplation. The former directs its creative activity toward the resistance of necessity in nature and society, and this struggle may, and often does, bring pain and suffering and requires sacrifice continuously. If conflict is the element of restlessness in creative freedom, then contemplation is the moment of rest. The contemplation of God is a free creative activity. Both the struggle and the contemplation are expressions of love, the former directed toward the world and the latter toward God. Contemplation provides the background against which the struggle acquires significance. Through contemplation man obtains temporary relief from the activism of existence, which always tends to tear him to pieces.[48]

It is very important to bear in mind that man's creative freedom, of which his ethical life is an integral part, is itself derived from the freedom of Christ by which man is redeemed and recreated. Every creative activity, intellectual, aesthetical, moral, and spiritual, says Berdyaev, brings to an end the world of necessity and initiates the new aeon. Such a creative activity of the new man, the transcendental man, is what Berdyaev often calls the *breakthrough* of metahistory into history. However, this business of transfiguring and transforming the world, both nature and society, must be seen from the perspective of Berdyaev's eschatology, from the purview of the End. Every creative act marks the dawn of the End of time and history. It is this free activity which makes man's eschatological anticipation creative, positive and dynamic. Through his creativeness, redeemed man injects meaning into life and history, and thus brings nearer the final con-

[48] *Ibid.*, p. 151 ff

summation of the new aeon. Berdyaev's eschatology is both heaven-bound and earth-bound. It unequivocally stresses what the new man can do and should do in this world to help bring about the climax of the historical process. This is his duty and obligation, and the purpose of the creative freedom conferred upon him by his Liberator. There is no utopian escapism into the other world.

To recapitulate, Berdyaev's philosophy develops around the existential paradox of freedom and necessity; essentially it culminates dialectically in a three-dimensional movement. This dialectic of freedom, however, is not theoretical but existential. It arises out of Berdyaev's own experience. As a human being, man possesses freedom as self-determination. This constitutes the thesis of the existential dialectic of freedom. Expressed negatively, this freedom of self-determination is simply the absence of all determination outside the self. As such, it may be described as being not anything at all. This means that man cannot possibly lose the potentiality within himself to say yes or no to events, people and God, regardless of the external determination he continues to experience in his life. Put positively, the freedom of self-determination is sheer voluntarism. This includes all psychological determination, conscious and unconscious, as both are part of the self. Freedom as self-determination, according to Berdyaev, is often irrational. As a capacity, it may create good or evil, and has frequently led man to slavery and misery. This initial freedom lacks the right directive, and needs to be liberated from its own selfishness. Another kind of freedom is necessary.

Freedom as self-perfection is the second form of freedom experienced and advocated by Berdyaev, the antithesis in his dialectic. This is rational freedom which consists in submission to the moral law. Through this submission and through knowledge of the truth, man hopes to advance on the road of self-perfection. In other words, freedom of self-perfection is acquired through reason. But perfection is never permanently and completely possessed because assimilation of the truth is never perfect in our historical existence and because obedience to the moral law tends to lead to compulsory virtue, which is actually a disguised form of slavery. Squarely across the landscape of this second freedom falls the shadow of human institutions forcing man to obey the moral law and impose the truth, often merely the alleged truth, upon him. Freedom as self-perfection, therefore, does not solve the problem of man's existence. Instead of respecting and supplementing man's freedom of self-determination, it violates and contradicts it. When either of these two freedoms attempts to exclude the other, the result is invariably the loss of freedom altogether. The pressing tension of thesis and antithesis must be resolved in a synthesis that can bring harmony and true freedom. This, according to Berdyaev, is accomplished through the living Truth of Christianity.

The freedom of Christ or Christian freedom is the third kind of freedom, in which the paradox is resolved. Only the Truth in Person can recognize the worth of the human personality and only through the redemptive work of the God-man, Jesus Christ, can the first two freedoms be reconciled and a freedom of self-realization and self-fulfillment be brought to man. This is possible because the God-man is both God and man in the absolute sense. The grace of Christ is the new force that illuminates the irrationality of the first freedom and restricts the coerciveness of the second. The crucified Christ does not impose Himself on anyone, Berdyaev reminds us. He makes His appeal to man's freedom of self-determination which He sanctifies in love and illuminates by the inner light of truth. In and through Christ, all humanity makes its response to God. The freedom which the Redeemer brings is freedom from guilt, freedom from fear of life and death, freedom from the grip of self-centeredness.

7

To be a Christian, according to Berdyaev, is to experience two processes, the one redemptive, and the other creative. The latter is derived from the former. A person who has been redeemed finds that a creative power is released in him. In other words, the redemptive process transforms and transfigures man himself. The creative process is the power by which man transforms and transfigures the world. Both are part and parcel of the Christian freedom of self-realization.

For Berdyaev, creativeness is first and foremost ethical in character. The ethics of creativeness is the creative freedom which the redemptive work of Christ ignites in the redeemed. Creative relations among people are relations saturated with the ideal Christian virtues. Creative activity in relation to things means a continuation of the work of the creation, as Berdyaev would say. But this too often involves working with people and, therefore, also has a moral content and is permeated by such attitudes as goodwill and cooperation, love and understanding, patience, and consideration. Man's creative activity is directed toward the realms of nature and society and, as such, calls for struggle. It is also directed toward God and, in this respect, takes the form of contemplation.

Redeemed man is the "new man," the "transcendental man," who has an important place in the scheme of things. It is here that Berdyaev views his existential dialectic of freedom from the perspective of his eschatology. Through his creative activity, the new man brings to an end, gradually and steadily, the realm of necessity and thus brings nearer the final consummation of the new aeon. He injects meaning into life and history, and thus the breakthrough of metahistory into history takes place. Berdyaev anticipates that the Second Coming of Christ will mark the beginning of the reign of true freedom in its qualitative and quantitative perfection. But the Christian is not passive in the meantime. He lives now an active, positive and dynamic life. He redeems the time, as Berdyaev says, with his free creative activity in all its aspects and forms: aesthetical, philosophical, social, ethical, and spiritual.

CHAPTER VIII

CRITICISMS AND EVALUATIONS

1 ONTOLOGY AND THEODICY

The main target of criticism in Berdyaev's philosophical thought has been his concept of *uncreated freedom* and, with it, the doctrine of the *Ungrund*, which he adopted from Jacob Boehme with some modifications. The objection is raised on the basis that an uncreated freedom, which goes into the making of man but whose source is other than God, implies an ontological dualism foreign to Christianity. According to the Christian view, the whole of man, including his freedom, has its origin in God. Furthermore, the theory of the *Ungrund* as a primordial principle or as the Divine Nothing out of which arises God and the cosmic entities also implies that God has a beginning and, therefore, cannot be eternal.

Evgueny Lampert called Berdyaev's uncreated freedom "the most disastrous conclusion in his whole philosophy, and one which seems in fact in no way warranted by his own fundamental presuppositions."[1] It is disastrous from the Christian viewpoint because it implies an ontological dualism.

Oliver Fielding Clarke questions the soundness of Lampert's conclusion. "How can it be unwarranted by Ber-

[1] Evgueny Lampert, "Nicolas Berdyaev," in Donald Attwater (ed.), *Modern Christian Revolutionaries* (New York: The Devin-Adair Co., 1947), p. 346, footnote 4

dyaev's 'fundamental presuppositions,'" Clarke argues, "when it is quite obviously itself one of those very same 'fundamental presuppositions'?" In Clarke's judgment, Berdyaev's *Ungrund* and, with it, uncreated freedom, does not lead to a metaphysical dualism because it is not a concept:

> It is not a part of a philosophical structure, nor is it a religious dogma. It is, so to speak, "metatheological." It is a basic intuition.[2]

But Clarke's sympathetic defense of Berdyaev does not clarify the meaning of uncreated freedom. The stigmatic ontological dualism of which Berdyaev has been accused is not convincingly invalidated. Clarke considers the *Ungrund* as one of Berdyaev's fundamental presuppositions and at the same time does not think it is part of Berdyaev's philosophical structure. But is not the presupposition logically a part of the philosophical structure which is erected on it? As a matter of fact, Clarke's interpretation of Berdyaev's *Ungrund* and uncreated freedom tends to support the existence of a metaphysical dualism. Says Clarke:

> This abyss is not part of God's creation, because it is prior to creation—it is the free nothing out of which God creates.[3]

Nothing is gained and hardly any light is shed on the problem by Clarke's closing statement:

> Anything could be. "With God all things are possible." Language disintegrates at this point, but those who will read and re-read Berdyaev on this subject will come to see his meaning.[4]

[2] Oliver Fielding Clarke, *Introduction to Berdyaev* (London: Geoffrey Bles, 1950), p. 87
[3] *Ibid.*, p. 87
[4] *Ibid.*

Clarke ends his chapter "Venture in Assessment" on the same note with which he began; it opens with the words: "The acid test to be applied to the work of any personalist philosopher is how far it succeeds in awakening the person who reads it." The validity of such a criterion is questionable. It is vaguely noncommittal and tends to put a personalist philosopher, like Berdyaev, at the mercy of the reader's possible intellectual and spiritual slumber and at the whims or excessiveness of his subjective feelings.

Another defender of Berdyaev is Michel A. Vallon, whose argument to refute the charge of ontological dualism takes a different direction. The expressions *Ungrund* and uncreated freedom, writes Vallon, are not concepts but symbols, which are not susceptible to rationalization. This is virtually what Berdyaev himself says. "All one can do," Vallon suggests, ". . . is to interpret them in the light of one's experience."[5] Vallon summarizes his position in the following statement:

> Berdyaev's own interpretation might be formulated as follows: I apprehend the ultimate reality neither in terms of monism nor of dualism but *as if* there were at the root of existence a basic antithesis, to wit, between God and uncreated freedom both of which, however, are transcended in the final mystery of the divine Godhead. He who will adapt this approach to Berdyaev's thought will alone gain access to its depth and significance.[6]

Would Berdyaev really formulate his interpretation of the dilemma in this manner? Would he accept the *as if* on which Vallon's statement hinges? Was not Berdyaev too existential to apprehend ultimate reality on the basis of an abstract assumption? Nowhere does Berdyaev give the im-

[5] Michel Alexander Vallon, *An Apostle of Freedom: Life and Teachings of Nicolas Berdyaev* (New York: Philosophical Library, 1960), p. 300

[6] *Ibid.*

pression that the antithesis between God and uncreated freedom was merely an assumption. To believe that it was is to attribute to him the sin of rationalization and conceptualization, against which he fought. The antithesis between God and uncreated freedom, whatever its meaning, was a concrete reality that Berdyaev experienced in his own life.

Furthermore, if the antithesis between God and uncreated freedom is only an assumption, why does it need to be transcended in the final mystery of the divine Godhead? Moreover, Vallon's advice that "he who will adapt this approach to Berdyaev's thought will alone gain access to its depth and significance" is too broad, general, and ambiguous.

Matthew Spinka points out the relatedness of Berdyaev's uncreated freedom to the problem of theodicy. Berdyaev thought that uncreated freedom, which gives rise to both good and evil, absolves God from the responsibility for evil and suffering in the world. Spinka challenges Berdyaev's conviction that if human freedom were God's gift that it would make Him "responsible for man's abuse of that freedom."[7] He is right in saying that "'uncreated freedom' . . . does not free God from responsibility for at least consenting to use the 'meonic' stuff in creation, although he knew it contained freedom."[8] The whole concept of uncreated freedom, Spinka concludes, is gnostic and not Christian.

Berdyaev was aware of the attacks which his concept of uncreated freedom had invited and the misinterpretations to which it was subjected, and frankly attributed to his own manner of thinking and writing much of the severe criticism and open accusation directed to the concept and

[7] Matthew Spinka, *Nicolas Berdyaev: Captive of Freedom* (Philadelphia: The Westminster Press, 1950), p. 121 f
[8] *Ibid.*

the ontological dualism it implies. He plainly tells us that he advocates neither an "ontological dualism" nor an "ontological monism." " 'Groundless freedom' does not imply a kind of ontological dualism, which affirms the existence of two spheres, viz., God and freedom."[9] He regards his philosophy as existential, and "existential philosophy cannot be ontological."[10] For him, as it is for Jaspers, the sphere of freedom is Existence, which is more primary than Being and precedes it. If uncreated freedom implies a dualism, then, according to Berdyaev, such dualism would be existential and not ontological, a dualism comprising God and man as the two experienced realities.

Increasingly through his life, the very term ontology became anathema to Berdyaev. "I arrived at a position," he writes in his autobiography, "which compelled me to reject ontology, or the science of Being, altogether."[11] This rejection of ontology implied that the term uncreated freedom was no longer ontological but existential in its connotation. When Berdyaev says "freedom is uncreated," he simply means that man is free only if his freedom is self-determined, that he is a subject only if he is not manipulated as if he were a "thing,"[12]

> "Uncreated freedom" is a limiting notion, describing symbolically a reality which does not lend itself to logical definition . . . Beyond the antithesis between God and uncreated freedom . . . there lies the divine, transcendent Mystery, in which all antithesis and all contradictions are removed, and attempts at expressing it in logical propositions become superfluous.[13]

In the light of the final meaning that Berdyaev assigned to "uncreated freedom," the accusation that he resorted to

[9] Berdyaev, *Dream and Reality*, p. 179
[10] Berdyaev, *Truth and Revelation*, p. 68
[11] Berdyaev, *Dream and Reality*, p. 98
[12] *Ibid.*, p. 288
[13] *Ibid.*

the concept of it, or that he overexalted human freedom, as Erich Klamroth has pointed out,[14] in order to solve the problem of theodicy can hardly be accepted as entirely accurate. In *The Destiny of Man*, Berdyaev did write that "theodicy should seek to justify God by accounting for the origin of the distinction between good and evil."[15] But even in the same context, he points to the direction in which he was moving:

> We cannot judge of God from our side of the distinction between good and evil . . . When we ask whether God is free to will evil we apply to Him the categories of our fallen world . . . God reveals Himself to us as the source of all values, as infinite love. Theodicy can judge only in the light of what God has revealed to us about Himself. It defends God against human conceptions of Him, against human slander.[16]

Berdyaev wrote this in 1931. But even as early as 1916 in *The Meaning of the Creative Act*, he wrote, "Christ is the only theodicy . . . We cannot believe in God if there is no Christ."[17] And later in *Slavery and Freedom*, published in 1939, Berdyaev was even more positive about the solution of the problem of theodicy. He states:

> The problem of theodicy is not solved by objectivizing thought in an objectivized world order. It is only solved on the

[14] Erich Klamroth, *Der Gedanke der ewigen Schöpfung bei Nikolai Berdiajew* (Hamburg-Bergstedt: Herbert Reich, Evangelischer Verlag G. m. b. H., 1963), p. 98: "*Um der Theodizee willen hatte er die menschliche Freiheit so stark hervorgehoben; sie sollte eine Entlastung Gottes sein, indem sie die volle Verantwortung für die Störungen in der Schöpfungswelt Gottes auf die eigenen Schultern nahm* (For the sake of theodicy, he [Berdyaev] strongly stressed human freedom and held it fully responsible for the disturbances in God's created world in order to free God from such responsibility)." Trans. by this writer.

[15] Berdyaev, *The Destiny of Man*, p. 43

[16] *Ibid.*

[17] Berdyaev, *The Meaning of the Creative Act*, p. 137

existential plane where God reveals Himself as freedom, love and sacrifice, where He suffers for man and strives together with man against the intolerable suffering of the world.[18]

God is a God Who suffers with the world and with men. He is crucified Love; He is a Liberator. The Liberator appears not as power but as Crucifixion.[19]

Berdyaev's concern, as an existentialist thinker, is not with ontology but with existence. Existence has priority over being. Being can realize itself only in existence. The concrete human experience is the primary thing. Man's thinking is the expression of his personal existence. This is especially true of Berdyaev himself. He exemplifies the dictum of Kierkegaard that "subjectivity, inwardness, is the truth," and that "the eternal and essential truth" is "the truth which has an essential relationship to an existing individual because it pertains essentially to existence."[20] Berdyaev practiced Dilthey's creed that the truth, as well as the meaningfulness, of any logical structure depends, in the final analysis, on whether it can be referred to some concrete experience.[21] He would subscribe to Stern's definition that "the person is living whole, individual, unique, striving toward goals, self-contained and yet open to the world around him, he is capable of having experience."[22] Without taking into consideration the fact that thinking is a function of life, and that thought and experience can-

18 Berdyaev, *Slavery and Freedom,* p. 89

19 *Ibid.,* p. 85

20 Kierkegaard, *Concluding Unscientific Postscript,* p. 183

21 Wilhelm Dilthey, *Gesammelte Schriften* (Leipzig and Berlin: Vols. I–IX and XI–XII, 1914–36; Vol. X, 1944), Vol. VII, 38, 126

22 William Stern, *General Psychology from the Personalistic Standpoint* (New York: The Macmillan Co., 1938), p. 70, trans. by Howard D. Spoerl from the German *Allgemeine Psychologie auf personalistischer Grundlage* (The Hague: Martinus Nijhoff, 1935)

not and should not be separated, Berdyaev himself could not be understood.

In order to gain insight into Berdyaev's solution of the problem of theodicy, we must penetrate into "the existential centre" of his "unrepeatable unique personality."[23] When he says that "the problem of theodicy . . . is only solved on the existential plane where God reveals Himself as freedom, love and sacrifice,"[24] he means that he himself has experienced in spirituality, in the inwardness of his existential center, the solution of the problem of theodicy. In his own spiritual experience, ignited by his faith in a crucified Redeemer Who suffers for man and enlists his creative effort against the wrong and suffering in the world, Berdyaev found the answer to the problem of reconciling evil and suffering in the world with the almighty power and supreme goodness of God.

Berdyaev wrote as an existentialist, and he must be read as such in order to be understood. Otherwise mistaken representations of his thinking will inevitably result. Such misrepresentation is easily detected in the brief account of F. H. Heinemann in *Existentialism and the Modern Predicament*. Under the heading "The Mystical Anarchist," which is, incidentally, one of Berdyaev's own descriptions of himself, Heinemann gives a rather negative picture of Berdyaev with a positive background. The sarcastic description of Berdyaev as "the *jumping philosopher*, or rather the master-springer who jumps to the end of all things"[25] is itself jumping to conclusions and betrays an inability to follow the winding movement of Berdyaev's thought.

[23] Berdyaev, *Slavery and Freedom*, p. 87
[24] *Ibid.*, p. 89
[25] F. H. Heinemann, *Existentialism and the Modern Predicament* (New York: Harper & Brothers, 1953), Harper Torchbooks (1958), p. 161

Moreover, Heinemann's concluding statement about Berdyaev as having "rejected this world, he cannot but accept an eschatological transformation"[26] and that he "is not a real genius because he did not understand that creation calls for industry and work"[27] is unrealistic and lacks substantial verification. For Berdyaev this world was too real to be simply rejected. His whole life was anything but an escape from the world; rather, he sought to transform and transfigure it. And is not his tremendous scholarly output the product of industry and work? It would be superfluous to quote Berdyaev with reference to the stress he placed on creative activity. He may not be a real genius, according to Heinemann's specifications, but he certainly did understand that "creation calls for industry and work." Man's role in this world is anything but passive. It is because man is free and his existence is creative that he can join God in the numerous tasks of creation.

2 FAITH AND REASON

The list of descriptions of Berdyaev's philosophical and religious position is long and colorful. He has been called a "religious philosopher," "personalist philosopher," "philosopher of freedom," "apostle of freedom," "fighter for freedom," "captive of freedom," "Christian anthropologist," "orthodox socialist," "universal thinker," "prophetic thinker," "rebellious prophet," "eschatological existentialist," "moral anarchist," "metaphysical anarchist," "mystical anarchist," "the second Socrates," and "the Philo of our age." Some of these designations Berdyaev himself used to describe his own philosophical thought. Could the wide variety of attempts to identify him and his thought be itself an indication of his versatility?

It would perhaps be helpful and revealing to consider

26 *Ibid.*, p. 159
27 *Ibid.*, p. 162

Berdyaev's own self-criticism and claims before we begin our assessment of his thinking. It is true that what a person believes himself to be and what in reality he is may not always be identical. Yet, what a person thinks of himself can be a valuable clue to his true self. Inasmuch as Berdyaev attempts to sum up his thought and to state his position in his autobiography, selections from this work are pertinent.

> I am . . . no theologian, but a "religious philosopher"—a bird rare, if not unknown, in Western Europe but, for better or for worse, rather prominent in Russia.[28]

> My philosophy has never been "scientific": rather it was prophetic and eschatological in manner and orientation.[29]

> I am . . . a believing, free thinker . . . My thought is deeply rooted in an initial act of faith.[30]

> My philosophy is informed with this faith and is born of spiritual experience.[31]

> I do not claim to have a scientific bent in the matter or manner of my thinking.[32]

> I regard my type of philosophy as "existential" . . . My vocation is to proclaim not a doctrine but a vision.[33]

Berdyaev theologizes but does not claim to be a theologian. He regards himself as a philosopher but not in the traditional, academic sense. "I work and desire to work by inspiration."[34] "I do not think that philosophy will ever be able to speak the truth if it does not take full account

[28] Berdyaev, *Dream and Reality*, p. 325
[29] *Ibid.*, p. 91
[30] *Ibid.*, p. 185
[31] *Ibid.*, p. 301
[32] *Ibid.*, p. 287
[33] *Ibid.*, p. 289
[34] *Ibid.*

of the mysterious element of inspiration."[35] Berdyaev's philosophy is not abstract and does not proceed from premises. It is deeply grounded in an initial act of faith and is born of spiritual experience. It is in this sense and for this reason that his philosophy is existential. It is both spiritual and intellectual, but the former lies at the root of the latter.

He shows a striking resemblance to the early Christian thinkers who regarded their theology as a type of philosophy. His conception of philosophy is very different from that of the academic philosophers; here he is more like the Greeks, whose philosophy had a strong religious sentiment. He resembles Tertullian, who, like Kierkegaard, opposed the application of rational understanding in matters of religion and revelation. Berdyaev's ideas about the New Man and the New Age, as well as his eschatological perspective, are reminiscent of Irenaeus, who also stressed man's moral freedom and thought of history as a dynamic movement in which man is "making progress day by day, and ascending toward the perfect, that is, approximating the uncreated One."[36]

Berdyaev's type of philosophy and manner of writing lead us to regard him as an heir of the early Christian philosophers, particularly Clement and Origen. Not only in his discussion of the thorny problem of freedom and bold defense of it but also in his appraisal of mystical contemplation as the highest point of the Christian life, Berdyaev may very well be considered a modern parallel to Clement of Alexandria. Origen's emphasis on man's freedom in his pre-existence, the freedom to choose the kind of individual he wants to be morally and spiritually, finds

[35] *Ibid.*, p. 290

[36] Irenaeus, *Against Heresies*, IV, 38:3; quoted by Richard Kroner, *Speculation and Revelation in the Age of Christian Philosophy* (Philadelphia: The Westminster Press, 1959), p. 61

its echo in Berdyaev's freedom of self-determination and particularly in his earlier description of it as uncreated freedom. The views of Origen and Berdyaev on universal salvation, that eventually all beings will be transformed and transfigured, also reflect significant similarities.

In his emphasis on the primacy of faith over reason, Berdyaev has some affinity to Augustine. No doubt, the degree of balanced equilibrium which Augustine was able to reach in harmonizing faith and thought remains unsurpassed. This early church father was not a dialectical thinker and could not tolerate any contradictions and inconsistencies. The affinity between the two lies in their stress on faith as a prelude to understanding, inwardness as the road to truth, and interior illumination as the work of grace. Dr. Kroner's observation that Augustine stands "midway between antiquity and modern times" and that "he is less philosophic in the technical sense because he is more existential and more guided by the 'logic of the heart' (Pascal)"[37] applies also to Berdyaev.

It is true that, in his writings and by his own testimony, Berdyaev gives the impression that he cast his vote for faith over reason, that quite early in his life he had requested reason to make ample room for faith. In a sense, Christian faith in him became the master of ceremonies, so to speak, and this set the tone for his entire philosophy. His spiritual experience became the usher which set out to guide all new philosophical ideas into their proper accommodations. Nevertheless, the paradox of faith and reason continued to cause difficulties and invite new efforts at harmonization. The kind of blend of faith and reason which Berdyaev achieves is of the nature of a truce rather than peace, a truce that frequently was only temporary. This is so because, by and large, Berdyaev con-

[37] Richard Kroner, *Speculation and Revelation in the Age of Christian Philosophy*, p. 115

tinued to approach ultimate reality through both the revelation of faith and the speculation of reason. It is the convergence of the two methods, the two tendencies, the religious and the philosophical, despite Berdyaev's heavy leaning toward the former, that has been an important factor in giving rise to divergencies of opinions about the main direction of his thought. The contradictions and inconsistencies, inevitable in any attempted truce between faith and reason, continued to be a characteristic quality of Berdyaev's thought, a matter which he neither denies or hides nor tries to explain away. He insists that this is unavoidable because it is a part of life itself.

> The contradictions and inconsistencies . . . are inherent in the very nature of the philosophy which I profess, and they cannot and should not be eliminated.[38]

> I have the courage to be inconsistent.[39]

Berdyaev's writings are turbulent on the surface. The reader must go beneath this surface, into the depth of his thinking to find a large measure of serenity and profundity. But here, too, one encounters ambiguous darkness and misleading undercurrents. To a sounding of what lies in the deep we now turn.

3 CHRISTIAN REALISM

Berdyaev's dialectic of freedom, our study leads us to conclude, is a theo-philosophical doctrine which gives expression to a unique type of Christian realism. It is his personal response to his own predicament and to the human situation, his existential answer to the paradox of freedom and necessity.

Berdyaev personally experienced the enslaving forces of nature, society, civilization, and history. He expounded

[38] Berdyaev, *Dream and Reality*, p. 285
[39] *Ibid.*, p. 305

freedom as a dynamic concept because he desperately needed and wanted freedom as a living reality. He became champion of freedom because he had little of it himself. Several of the factors in Berdyaev's life that encroached on his personal freedom have already been indicated. For one thing, he could do nothing about the thorn in his flesh, that uncontrollable and unpredictable nervous condition with which he was afflicted from childhood. This condition, a *tic douloureux*, whose sudden attack disfigured him, no doubt caused him considerable embarrassment and discomfort in public and much anxiety and sadness in private. He had no freedom in the face of this fact which he considered an unexplainable and mysterious necessity of nature. He also experienced the fateful blow of history. Permanent separation from his homeland was a historical inevitability. The freedom to live in his own country and with his own Russian people was denied him. His freedom of self-determination, he had come to realize, was impotent to cope with the determinism of historical circumstances. This initial freedom, as it was shown earlier, is itself unpredictable and unreliable; it is irrational. Man's self-determination may lead him to slavery. People often exchange this freedom for security. Berdyaev's analysis and understanding of the ways by which man seeks to escape the grip of necessity are penetrating. His self-determination, by itself, lacks the inner directive and the inner illumination.

Berdyaev is also well-grounded in what he says about the second freedom, the freedom of self-perfection. Necessity cannot be overcome by man's self-determination, his human freedom. Man, therefore, attempts to defeat it by his self-perfection, his ethical freedom. According to Berdyaev, this is historically true in the life of the individual. Greek and Old Testament religions are examples of man seeking to defeat necessity through the freedom of self-perfection, which he hoped to realize simply through obedience to the moral law. Berdyaev is veracious in showing that submission to the law leads to forced virtue, which is a form of slavery. He repeatedly warns against the tyranny to which the second freedom leads, by referring to Dostoyevsky's image of the Grand Inquisitor, symbol of the organized institution, which ignores man's initial freedom.

The first and second freedoms, as a thesis and antithesis, can be resolved only in the Christian synthesis, the freedom of self-realization. Christian freedom, which is the gift of the God-man, Jesus Christ, and which redeems man and thereby renders him creative, is the only solution. Berdyaev's writing about the creative activity or *the ethics of creativeness,* in which the redeemed man engages, constitutes one of his major contributions. For him, to be created in God's image means to be "a created creator." Through Redemption man is transfigured and elevated from being merely human, a creature, the result of falling away from God, to being again divine-human, a created creator. To be redeemed means to be restored to the status of co-creator with God. According to Berdyaev, creativity is fundamentally a religious matter. It lies at the very heart of man's relation to God and his response to divine love.[40] Artistic and scientific creativity, in Berdyaev's opinion, is secondary to, and derivative from, creativity in the religious sense.[41]

In a materialistic civilization which tends to conceive of creativity in terms of productivity, Berdyaev's refined conception of free creativity proves to be a sound and welcome emphasis. In his sense, creativity is not necessarily tangible output, but first and foremost contemplation and receptivity, which are basic in the spiritual experience. In a culture that tends to overvalue physical labor, Berdyaev

[40] Berdyaev, *Dream and Reality,* p. 207
[41] *Ibid.*

stresses the significance of man's creative thinking. Directed toward this world, man's creative activity implies a struggle with the forces of necessity for the purpose of transfiguring it. Every moment of creative activity means a victory of freedom over necessity. Every such victory brings nearer the final transfiguration of the world.

Erich Klamroth seems to overlook this kind of progress when, in assessing Berdyaev's concept of creativity he writes: "*Ein Fortschritt im Weltprozess ist nicht wahrnehmbar; alle menschliche schöpferische Anstrengung ist zum Scheitern verurteilt*[42] (No progress in world process can be observed; all human creative effort is doomed to failure)." Such a view undervalues the inner liberation that man experiences as a result of his creative activity. "The awakening of creative energy," says Berdyaev, "is inner liberation and is accompanied by a sense of freedom."[43] Is it really true and accurate to conclude, as Klamroth does, that human creativeness, according to Berdyaev, finally leads to a dead end, to a "fiasco"?[44] Does Berdyaev's "ethics of creativeness" in relation to other people, which expresses itself in acts of "love, of pity, of help, of peacemaking,"[45] have no value at all? Klamroth does not take into consideration Berdyaev's basic principle that, "All creativeness is love and all love is creative"?[46] Similarly, Zenkovsky's verdict that Berdyaev's "sincere and profound moral passion degenerated into an 'ethic of creativity', indifferent to reality," and that "the chief reason for this self-sterilization of Berdyaev's thought lay in his *romanticism*, his constant readiness to repudiate reality" seems to be unfair, lacking documented verification in the

[42] Erich Klamroth, *Der Gedanke der ewigen Schöpfung bei Nikolai Berdiajew*, p. 96
[43] Berdyaev, *The Destiny of Man*, p. 147
[44] Klamroth, *op. cit.*, p. 95
[45] Berdyaev, *The Destiny of Man*, p. 148
[46] *Ibid.*, p. 141

brief survey in which it appears.[47] One wonders what Zenkovsky meant by the "reality" which Berdyaev is supposed to have repudiated and to which he was indifferent. And "reality" by whose definition? Zenkovsky's assessment is hopelessly weakened by its own vague generalization. In the course of our study, we have come to know that Berdyaev was far from being indifferent to reality of any kind, particularly "the world of love" which he called "the world of reality."[48]

From the Christian point of view, Berdyaev is also sound in his eschatological perspective. He maintains that it is possible not to be a victim of either optimism or pessimism. The perfect resolution of the paradox of freedom and necessity is not realized within the confines of history. It must await the Second Coming of Christ and the perfect reign of the Kingdom of God. This eschatological orientation, however, does not carry within it a potential degeneration into passivism during this life. On the contrary, the eternal hope of the Christian and his momentary experience of freedom as self-realization places upon him the responsibility to engage in creative activity, which is fundamentally spiritual and ethical, and which is an important factor in bringing about the End of history and the culmination of the new aeon. Berdyaev, we may say, is a realistic metahistorian. He was convinced that history as a province of necessity was constantly being penetrated by metahistorical forces that inject meaning into this world. Through his firm belief in the ultimate realization of the purposes of God, he was able to look into the future with hope and anticipate the final victory of freedom over necessity.

Berdyaev's keen sense of history and metahistory, but-

[47] V. V. Zenkovsky, *A History of Russian Philosophy*, Vol. II, p. 780

[48] Berdyaev, *The Destiny of Man*, p. 187

tressed by a quiet spiritual experience and reinforced by a
vivid imagination, provided him with the necessary quali-
fications to speak with a prophetic voice. But prophecy in
him had to be expressed and communicated through a
philosophical language. This was perhaps a matter of expediency. Because he does this, he can be heard by our
modern age. He saw both the dangers and the weaknesses
of modern civilization. He perceived the dehumanization
caused by industry and technology. He foresaw the evil
results of the Russian Revolution and lived to witness the
fulfillment of his predictions. But Berdyaev was not a
prophet of doom. He was a prophet of free creative activity
and foresaw the dawn of a new era, which he described in
The New Middle Ages. In this new age, the same creative
forces which operated in the Middle Ages, but which have
been dormant, will prevail. Berdyaev looked beyond history and believed in the ultimate redemption of all
creation.

4 HUMANISTIC TENDENCIES

Berdyaev's firm belief in universal salvation and the
eventual victory of good for all mankind is in line with the
conviction of the Orthodox Church. But with his stress on
the freedom of the individual to determine his own destiny, it seems rather strange that he accepted this doctrine
of universal salvation without reservations or modifications. The theological basis of the doctrine lies in the
belief that all mankind participated in a mystical way in
Christ's work of salvation. To the biblical statement that
"God was in Christ reconciling the world unto Himself"
Berdyaev would add that "man was in Christ reconciling
God unto himself." In *Freedom and the Spirit,* he writes:

> In Christ human nature co-operates with the work of Re-
> demption . . . Redemption is a dual process in which both

God and man share . . . Without human nature and the exercise of human freedom it would be impossible.[49]

Berdyaev's overemphasis on the active role which mankind plays in Redemption through its mystical identification with the human nature of Christ lacks the adequate scriptural support and betrays some hidden humanistic tendencies. This undue stress on the human aspect of Redemption tends to dilute the doctrine of Incarnation into a doctrine of cooperation. According to the New Testament, it is God who was in Christ and who took the initiative and put on "the form of a servant"; man is not a co-agent but an object of Redemption. He shares in the Redemption of mankind not as a subject but as a potential recipient. Berdyaev's stress on the equality of the human and the divine in the work of salvation, a stress that is, of course, foreign to the Orthodox Church, tends to convert the work of Christ's Redemption into a cooperative process that takes place halfway between God and man with God descending, so to speak, and man ascending to some meeting point in the middle.

Furthermore, one detects in Berdyaev's understanding of Christ's Redemption of mankind and the belief in universal salvation a disguised form of determinism. This is despite Berdyaev's emphasis that the grace of Christ illuminates man's freedom of self-determination from within. How can man be free and responsible if his freedom of self-determination is mysteriously conditioned from within and, through its mystical union with the God-man, makes an affirmative response to God? And if all mankind, through its mystical union with the God-man, makes an affirmative response to God, not merely potentially but actually, how do we explain the lack of actual response to God in the lives of millions?

Berdyaev deserves all admiration for defending man's

[49] Berdyaev, *Freedom and the Spirit*, p. 177

freedom, personality and dignity. But he arouses our suspicion in his overexultation of man and his making him a little higher than the angels. It is this humanistic leaning that drives Berdyaev to reject any principle of atonement in the work of salvation and to be "much more sensitive to evil than to sin."[50] To explain the doctrine of atonement away by saying that it is nothing but the projection of human standards of justice and earthly court procedures into the divine level and ignore the whole question of divine justice seems to contradict Scriptural revelation, which Berdyaev professes to have accepted as his guide.

Apparently the influence of Jacob Boehme continued to be an undercurrent in Berdyaev's thought. Despite his efforts to baptize the doctrine of the *Ungrund* into the Christian faith and to reinterpret it in the Christian light, it continued to present a potential danger to basic Christian beliefs about God and the creation. Under the cover of mysticism and in spite of Berdyaev's move from ontology to ethics, Boehme's theory of the *Ungrund* never completely ceased to inject humanistic elements into his thinking.

From the Christian point of view, the doctrine of the *Ungrund* and Berdyaev's later interpretation of it, as well as his attempts to equate it with the "divine nothing" of Dionysius should be rejected. There is no evidence of the independent existence of a nothing which God utilizes for creating the world. It would be more accurate to say that *nothingness* has no existence except as a concept in man's mind. To say that God created the world "out of nothing" means simply that He brought forth all that exists besides Himself, including man and his will, as entities that are ontologically new.

The humanistic bent in Berdyaev's thought, which finds an expression in his concept of human freedom as self-

[50] Berdyaev, *Dream and Reality*, p. 174

determination, should not be attributed only to Western European influences but also to Russian humanism, with its twofold stress on mysticism and universalism. Berdyaev is a prominent star in a galaxy of Russian religious philosophers who are known for their attempts to work out a Christian *Weltanschauung*. He belongs to what is known as the Russian Religious Renaissance of the Twentieth Century[51] which is a "religious and artistic revival among the Russian intelligentsia" that revised its "previous negative attitude to Christianity and recognized the intrinsic significance of the Orthodox Church."[52] This movement, which may be traced back to the early Slavophiles, includes such thinkers as Sergius Bulgakov, Peter Struve, Simeon Frank, Vasily Zenkovsky, Vladimir Lossky, Fedor Stepun and Nicolas Zernov. Their efforts to bring about religious, social, and political renewal in Russia began early in the twentieth century, were arrested and reversed by the Communists, but found currency among the Russians in exile in western Europe. Most of these philosophers were driven out of Russia and some perished in Russian prisons. Several of them succeeded in developing systems of Christian philosophy, but mostly because of their humanism, some of their theories were alien to the thinking of the Orthodox Church. This is quite true of Berdyaev, who found it difficult to embrace the Orthodox belief without reservation as it conflicted with his understanding of, and emphasis on, human freedom. "I cannot, in all conscience, call myself a typical 'orthodox' of any kind."[53] "As far back as I can remember there has been something uneasy, pained, divided in my relations with

[51] A recent study of this movement was made by Nicolas Zernov, *The Russian Religious Renaissance of the Twentieth Century* (New York: Harper & Row, 1963); cf. also V. V. Zenkovsky, *A History of Russian Philosophy*, Vol. II, pp. 754–91

[52] Nicolas Zernov, *op. cit.*, p. vii f

[53] Berdyaev, *Dream and Reality*, p. 177

the Orthodox Church."[54] In the words of Zernov, "Berdyaev neither apostatized from the Church, nor returned to it as a prodigal son."[55]

5 CHRISTIAN EXISTENTIALISM

Berdyaev conceived of life not as a problem to be solved but as a reality to be experienced. His concern is focused upon the whole personality. For him, the ultimate issues of life and death have an existential significance. Not the world of things but the concrete human experience constitutes the heart of his philosophical concern. His thinking revolves around "the unrepeatable unique personality of an existential centre."[56] His life and thought were a call to freedom of complete self-realization through a redemptive co-creativity with God.

As an existential thinker, Berdyaev is far removed from such contemporary existentialists as Heidegger, Jaspers, and Sartre, and is more in the tradition of Pascal and Kierkegaard. Some years ago, within the context of a discussion reported by Jean Wahl, Berdyaev described Kierkegaard's existentialism as "expressionist,"[57] as an expression of existence, in an effort to distinguish it from that of the systematized existentialists. For Berdyaev, as it is for Kierkegaard, the Christian faith is the answer to the tragedy of human existence and the answer to the problem of freedom. Among his contemporaries, Berdyaev has the closest affinity with Gabriel Marcel, who conceives of freedom in terms of "creative receptivity."[58] Berdyaev devotes a few

[54] Berdyaev, *Dream and Reality*, p. 174

[55] Nicolas Zernov, *op. cit.*, p. 154

[56] Berdyaev, *Slavery and Freedom*, p. 87

[57] Jean Wahl, *A Short History of Existentialism*, trans. by Forrest Williams and Stanley Maron (New York: Philosophical Library, 1949), p. 56

[58] Lecture at the University of Pennsylvania, November 25, 1961

pages in his autobiography to his associations with Marcel and with the "personalists'" meetings in Paris. Both Berdyaev and Marcel consider creativity as the basic role of man, who serves as a vehicle of God's creation. Man finds self-fulfillment through his creativity. Marcel writes:

> What distinguishes the free act is that it helps to make me what I am, as a sculptor might carve me, whereas the contingent or insignificant act, the act which might just as well have been performed by anybody, has no contribution to make to this sort of creation of myself by myself.[59]

In spite of his humanistic tendencies, Berdyaev's *Weltanschauung* is essentially Christian. Underlying his Christian world conception is the conviction that spiritual freedom, which Christ, the God-man, offers, is the only reliable freedom. A significant feature of his thought is the belief that Christianity alone is the religion of freedom because it is at heart a religion of love. Berdyaev deserves credit for his struggle against all ideologies that attempt to replace Christian values. He convincingly showed "how little good there is in goodness" in the life of the individual and society, outside and within the church. Like the ancient prophet Amos, Berdyaev denounced with courage, insight and vigor, the injustices and dangers of his times. He shed light on the biblical truth that everything that is earthly must pass away and that the Kingdom of God alone will stand.

One of the outstanding aspects of Berdyaev's achievements is his ability to express the Christian truth in an original way that has stimulated and will continue to stimulate interest in Christianity in hearts and minds that otherwise would remain closed to it.[60] Obviously, Ber-

[59] Gabriel Marcel, *The Mystery of Being* (Chicago: The Henry Regnery Company, 1951), Vol. II, p. 117
[60] Cf. N. O. Lossky, *History of Russian Philosophy* (New York: International Universities Press, Inc., 1951), p. 250.

dyaev does not solve the deep mystery of Christianity, but
he does succeed in clearing up much of the debris of historical Christianity that has stood in the way of many an
honest mind. He has vividly shown how man, even Christian man, is tempted to create God in his own image, not
only the best but also the worst of his images of himself.
Our conception of God has often been stamped with our
own anthropomorphism, cosmomorphism, and sociomorphism. Berdyaev points, for instance, to the patriarchal
conception of God as arising out of the social relationships
that existed in the family at the time that conception was
formed. He explains how the master-slave relations in
social life have been projected into the relations between
God and man.

It was chiefly because of Berdyaev's persistence that
"God is Mystery"[61] whose knowledge eludes our understanding that he has been accused of gnosticism. But these
accusations often overlook the fact that Berdyaev's episte-
mology is mystical and that God who cannot be grasped
by man's mind is, nevertheless, accessible through mystical
communion.

> God is Mystery, a Mystery towards which man transcends
> and with which he enters into communion . . . Contacts with
> God and communion with Him are possible.[62]

Berdyaev's philosophic thought may be regarded as a
bridge between Russian and Western thinking. The time
may come when it may be recognized as such and thus
contribute toward bringing the East and West somewhat
closer together. Particularly his concepts of freedom and
creativity and his stress on the worth and dignity of the

Lossky, who knew Berdyaev for many years and was exiled from
Russia with him in 1922, gives a brief survey and a fair assessment of Berdyaev's philosophic thought.

[61] Berdyaev, Slavery and Freedom, p. 83
[62] Ibid., p. 83

human personality can serve as guideposts for modern man and his technological civilization and as a common platform for both East and West.[63]

In an age that yearns and struggles for freedom, Berdyaev carries the torch of spiritual freedom and points to the true Liberator of mankind, the God-man, Jesus Christ, as the only agent through Whom it may be secured. Berdyaev's understanding of ethics as a creative activity that has its source in genuine spiritual experience has a sparkling quality of realism. As a Christian existentialist, he has demonstrated the fact that living life in co-creativity with God is more important than theorizing about it. Through this free creative activity ethical values are generated.

Through his mystical personalism, Berdyaev is a champion of human personality and a defender of its inalienable right to spiritual freedom. In a world that is striving for world harmony, his prophetic voice warns against the enslaving forces of such a harmony. The idea of the harmony of the whole world, Berdyaev believed, is the power of objectification over human existence. It is a part of the realm of necessity, and, therefore, can have no meaning. World harmony that is dictated and implemented by the pressures of pragmatic necessity, whether political, economic or cultural, deprives man of his freedom and uses him as a means to an end. This does not mean that Berdyaev is opposed to world unity. On the contrary, he is a firm believer in universalism.

[63] Cf. Fedor Stepun, *Mystische Weltschau: Fünf Gestalten des russischen Symbolismus* (München: Carl Hanser Verlag, 1964), p. 198 f. This work, which contains a chapter on Berdyaev, came to the attention of this writer after the present study had been completed. Stepun, a personal friend of Berdyaev, gives a penetrating interpretation of the dominant themes in Berdyaev's philosophy, including objectification, symbolism, mysticism, freedom, and creativity.

To be frank, I dislike the very term "foreigner" or "alien" with all its evil undertones and overtones, and I cannot put my-self in the position of distinguishing human beings according to their nationality. Every "foreigner" is my compatriot.[64]

World unity, in Berdyaev's view, can be attained only from within through practicing and spreading spiritual freedom which is the gift of Christ. "The Church uni-versal, which knows neither East nor West, is the spiritual basis for the unity of mankind."[65] Only a world unity that is built on the solid foundation of Christian freedom is able to safeguard the freedom and dignity of human personality because it has its source in God Who "is al-ways in freedom, never in necessity, always in personality, never in the world whole."[66]

"God is the Meaning of human existence."[67]

[64] Berdyaev, *Dream and Reality*, p. 265
[65] Berdyaev, *The Realm of Spirit and the Realm of Caesar*, p. 159
[66] Berdyaev, *Slavery and Freedom*, p. 87
[67] *Ibid.*

Subjectivism and Individualism in Social Philosophy. St. Petersburg: Popov, 1901. In this first major philosophic work, Berdyaev attempts to reconcile Marxism and idealism at a period
when he was moving from the former to the latter; he attacks
the materialistic implications of Marxism and advocates the
absolute priority of beauty, goodness, and truth. With this
work, Berdyaev emerges as the leader of the movement that
subsequently has been called From Marxism to Idealism.

The New Religious Consciousness and Society. St. Petersburg:
Pirozhkov, 1907. This book represents Berdyaev's early views
on religious anarchism. He later regarded it as quite inadequate.

The Spiritual Crisis of the Intelligentsia. St. Petersburg: Obschest-
vennaya Polza, 1910. This volume marks Berdyaev's initial step
from idealism toward a religious philosophy. It contains his
prophetic thoughts about the Russian Revolution, among these
his intuitive expectation that the Revolution was not going to
mean a victory for freedom.

Philosophy of Freedom. Moscow: Put, 1911. This work docu-
ments. Berdyaev's first effort to deal with the problem of theodicy, the attempt to reconcile the fact of evil and suffering in
this world with the belief in an omnipotent and merciful God.
Here Jacob Boehme's influence on Berdyaev can be noticed
clearly for the first time. Because of Berdyaev's emphasis that
philosophy be freed from rationalism and placed in the service

of man's religious life, this volume may be regarded as a trail blazer in modern existentialism.

A. S. Khomyakov. Moscow: Put, 1912. Berdyaev wrote this book as a tribute to Khomyakov (1804–60), one of the elder Slavophiles and a lay theologian of the Orthodox Church. Khomyakov's stress on freedom as the heartbeat of Christianity and his conception of the church as a non-authoritarian "organic togetherness" (*sobornost*) made a deep and lasting impression on Berdyaev's thinking.

The Meaning of the Creative Act. Moscow, 1916. Translation by Donald A. Lowrie. New York: Harper & Brothers, 1955. This book marks an important milestone in Berdyaev's philosophic development. It contains the blueprints of his religious philosophy and is based on the thesis that, as a co-creator with God, man makes a vital contribution toward the ultimate victory of freedom over necessity. The concept of creativity is analyzed in its relation to culture, morals, beauty, love, sex, and mysticism.

The Fate of Russia. Moscow: Leman & Sacharov,. 1918. In this book, the last of Berdyaev's works to be published in Russia, he voiced his opinion concerning the leading part which he thought Russia would have to play in postwar Europe. The book is permeated by an attitude of optimistic anticipation of an eventual international cooperation.

The Meaning of History. Berlin, 1923. Translation by George Reavey. London: Geoffrey Bles, 1936; New York: Scribner's, 1936. This work grew out of a series of lectures delivered in Moscow at the Liberal Academy of Spiritual Culture in 1919–20. The Epilogue, "The Will to Life and to Culture," was written in 1922. In this book, Berdyaev expounds the basic principles of a Christian philosophy of history. "The Meaning of Tradition," "Time and Eternity," "The Destiny of the Jews," "The Renaissance and Humanism," and "The Doctrine of Progress and the Goal of History" are discussed.

The World-Outlook of Dostoyevsky. Prague, 1923. *Dostoyevsky.* Translation by Donald Attwater. New York: Sheed & Ward, 1934. This rather slim volume is a penetrating interpretation of Dostoyevsky, to whom Berdyaev felt deeply indebted. Dostoyevsky's ideas on freedom, spirit, love, evil, Russia, and revolution are expounded. As Berdyaev himself tells us in *Dream and Reality* (p. 231), the writing of the book was inspired by the religious and social implications of the "Legend of the Grand Inquisitor" in *The Brothers Karamazov*.

The Philosophy of Inequality. Berlin: Obelisk, 1923. In this work, Berdyaev severely and boldly criticizes the Russian Revolution and vehemently and passionately denounces the Communist regime. He expresses his concern for freedom over against the slavery introduced by the new Russian rulers, and advocates the worth and dignity of the human personality as the only basis for true social equality.

The New Middle Ages. Berlin: Obelisk, 1924. *The End of our Time.* Translation by Donald Attwater. New York: Sheed & Ward, 1933. This book became a "best seller" and was translated into a dozen languages. In it Berdyaev attempts to show that World War I marked the end of modern times and the beginning of what he calls the New Middle Ages in which he prophetically anticipates a return to the religious beliefs associated with the medieval spirit. This means the end of humanism and liberalism. In the new era, an increasingly important part will be played by the intellect.

Philosophy of the Free Spirit. Paris, 1927. *Freedom and the Spirit.* Translation by Oliver Fielding Clarke. New York: Scribner's, 1935. Although Berdyaev writes in the introduction to this volume that it is "not a theological work," it is the most theological of his books. The original title is an indication that he meant it to be philosophical in nature. Perhaps it may justly be regarded as a "theo-philosophical" work, in which Berdyaev attempts to set forth for the first time the fundamental principles of his religious existential philosophy. He urges that philosophy be divorced from rationalism and "become a founda-

8

tion of the religious life." The starting point of both theology
and philosophy, Berdyaev stresses, is neither with God nor
with man but with the God-man. Sharp criticism is directed
against abstract metaphysics and against the Church as an institution. This work, in which the mystical element is quite
strong, places a special emphasis on the divine quality of human energy. The French edition of it earned Berdyaev the
French Academy prize in moral and religious sciences.

The Destiny of Man. Paris: YMCA-Press, 1931. Translation by
Natalie Duddington. New York: Scribner's, 1935; London:
Geoffrey Bles, 1935. This is one of the most valuable and most
systematic of Berdyaev's books, in which his moral orientation
reaches a stable climax of development. As the subtitle indicates, it is "An Essay on Paradoxical Ethics." Part I opens
with a critical inquiry into the problem of ethical knowledge,
then deals with the origin of good and evil, and concludes with
a discussion of Berdyaev's own philosophical anthropology. In
Part II, Berdyaev develops his theory of ethics, the Ethics of
Creativeness, which supersedes, in his opinion, the Ethics of
Law and the Ethics of Redemption. The following areas of
ethical concern, among others, are pin-pointed and analyzed:
"Conscience and Freedom," "Fear, Terror and Anguish,"
"Love and Compassion," and "The State, Revolution and
War." Part III deals with "The Last Things" and with
"Eschatological Ethics."

Russian Religious Psychology and Communist Atheism. Paris:
YMCA-Press, 1931. *The Russian Revolution.* Translation by
Donald Attwater. New York: The Macmillan Co., 1932. In
this work, Berdyaev tries to assess Communism: its weakness
and strength, its negative and positive aspects. The Communist
denial of God led to the depreciation of man. The social collective takes the place of both God and man. This means the
suppression of personal conscience, reason and freedom. Berdyaev's rejection of Communism is based on spiritual, not eco-
nomic-political grounds. He discusses certain positive contributions of Communism, at least in theory, with which he is in
sympathy: a planned economy that demands work from every
individual according to his ability and compensates him ac-

cording to his need; an end to the exploitation of man by man; and the attempt to eliminate class struggle and war by creating a classless society.

"I" and the World of Objects. Paris: YMCA-Press, 1934. *Solitude and Society*. Translation by George Reavey. London: Geoffrey Bles, 1938. This is perhaps the most philosophical of Berdyaev's books and the most existential of his philosophical writings. It is one of his best and most original creations. The Russian title is more expressive of its existential character than the title of the translation. In his autobiography, Berdyaev says that he could have very well called it *The Sociology of Knowledge*. The work opens with an epistemological study of philosophy as a discipline that occupies a place between religion and science. After a penetrating discussion of the Existential Subject and the Process of Objectification, Berdyaev deals with the problem of knowledge, which for him is not merely a matter of logic but depends also on the extent and intensity of communion and communication between men. In the fourth chapter, the paradox of time in its relation to anxiety, creativity, knowledge, change and eternity is discussed. The book closes with an analysis of personality and its interaction with the natural, social and cultural milieu.

The Fate of Man in the Modern World. Paris, 1934. Translation by Donald A. Lowrie. New York: Morehouse Publishing Co., 1935. This work has enjoyed a well-deserved popularity and has been translated into seven languages. It represents a revised interpretation of the philosophy of modern history which Berdyaev discussed earlier in *The New Middle Ages* (*The End of our Time*). The "dehumanization" of man by Fascism, Naziism, Communism, capitalism, technology, and war is vividly described and masterfully analyzed. Berdyaev does not hesitate to allocate to the organized Christian Church its share of blame in bringing about the depersonalization of man. He stresses the need for "a new Christian piety" upon which depends "the fate of man in the modern world."

Spirit and Reality. Paris, 1937. Translation by George Reavey. London: Geoffrey Bles, 1939. The doctrine of God-manhood is

expounded in this work. The concept "spirit" as understood by
the Greeks, Romans, Hebrews and Indians, and as used in the
philosophies of Kant, Hegel, Fichte, Hartman, Jaspers, and
Karl Barth is discussed in detail. Berdyaev delineates the conviction that "spirituality" is not in opposition to the "body" but
instead seeks the body's transfiguration, the process by which
the highest qualities in man are realized. The roles of symbolization, creativity, and mysticism in bringing about the liberation of the Spirit from objectification are analyzed. One chapter is devoted to "Evil and Suffering as Problems of Spirit."

The Origin of Russian Communism. London: Geoffrey Bles,
1937. Berdyaev wrote this book to refute the belief, which
found currency especially in the West, that Communism and
Christianity are compatible. After a historical survey of the ori-
gins of Communism, he shows that the two have nothing in
common and that Christianity alone can protect the world from
the danger of Communism.

Slavery and Freedom. Paris, 1939. Translation by R. M. French.
New York: Scribner's, 1939. In this volume, Berdyaev first re-
views his "philosophical journey" and acknowledges his debt
to the thinkers by whom he was influenced. Then he goes on
to analyze the natural, economic, political, technological, and
spiritual forces that enslave man. He is outspoken in his indignant criticism of the forms of government and society which
deprive man of his freedom whether they be Fascist, Communist or bourgeois. In his opinion, the liberation of the human
spirit is contingent upon a fuller realization of the human personality. Berdyaev makes it emphatic throughout the book that
only personality, the highest of all values, can solve social
problems.

The Russian Idea. Paris, 1946. Translation by R. M. French.
New York: The Macmillan Co., 1948. In this book, Berdyaev
gives expression to his belief in the messianic vocation of "Holy
Russia," which is "above all else bound up with the social transformation of the world" (p. 2). He evaluates his own contribution to the Russian Religious-Philosophical Renaissance and explains why he considers himself one of the creators of Russian

religious philosophy. He also expounds the Orthodox doctrine of the gradual perfecting of man by a process of divinization.

The Existential Dialectic of the Divine and the Human. Paris, 1947. *The Divine and the Human.* Translation by R. M. French. London: Geoffrey Bles, 1949. This book was written during 1944–45 and is the result of reflection on the devastation of World War II. It contains an exposition of the doctrine of God-manhood against the background of the experiences of fear, evil, suffering, beauty, spirituality and the hope of immortality. Berdyaev stresses the fact that "God is present in freedom and love, in truth and right and in beauty, and in the face of evil and wrong. He is present not as a judge and avenger but as appraisal and as conscience" (p. 8).

Toward a New Epoch. Translation from the original French (*Au seuil de la nouvelle époque.* Delachaux & Niestle S.A., Neuchatel, 1948) by Oliver Fielding Clarke. London: Geoffrey Bles, 1949. The main theme of this book of essays, as Berdyaev writes in the preface, is "the present world-crisis and the role which Russia plays in it." Written from the point of view of a philosophy of history, the essays present his conception of the new epoch toward which the postwar world is moving as "a new form of democracy, social democracy" (p. 115). In Berdyaev's view, Russia will contribute toward the transformation of the world and life through its universal outlook and eschatological orientation. The Christian Church will play a decisive role in the shaping of the new epoch, but, first, it must itself undergo a social revolution. "The part to be played by Christianity will certainly be enormous on condition that its old fictitious forms are left behind and that its prophetic aspect is revealed as the source of a different attitude toward the social problem" (p. 117). This work is a helpful source for understanding the history of Europe and Russia in the postwar years.

Essay on Eschatological Metaphysics. Paris, 1947. *The Beginning and the End.* Translation by R. M. French. London: Geoffrey Bles, 1952; New York: Harper & Brothers, 1952. In this vol-

ume, Berdyaev attempts to sum up his philosophical position
and surveys all metaphysical and existential problems in the
light of his eschatology. He defines his brand of existentialism
and indicates the main features of his philosophies of history
and religion. Part I traces his affinity to German idealism and
mysticism and discusses the dualities of nature and freedom,
object and subject, appearances and "things-in-themselves"
(Kant). In Part II, Berdyaev investigates the concept of Being
in its relation to objectification, existence, non-being, spirit,
and value. Part III constitutes an inquiry into the origin of evil
and an analysis of time, evolution, progress, necessity, fate,
freedom and creativity. Part IV deals with the problem of history and time as well as the nature of society, culture and civilization.

Self-knowledge, An Essay in Philosophical Autobiography. Translation by Katherine Lampert from the Russian and published in
English as *Dream and Reality.* London: Geoffrey Bles, 1950;
New York: The Macmillan Co., 1951. This *Philosophical Autobiography,* a work of frank self-analysis and critical self-assess-
ment, may be considered the crowning achievement of Berdyaev's literary creations. It was written mostly during the
turmoil of the early part of the Second World War and is sup-
plemented by two brief chapters composed after the war's end.
Berdyaev tells us in the preface that the book is not meant to
be an autobiography in the ordinary sense. In this essay on
"Self-knowledge," "I call my self and my life into question and
make them the object of critical enquiry." Here Berdyaev tries
to trace and understand the history of his mind and the development of his philosophical thought. He is not interested in
presenting the facts of his life but rather in his own creative reaction to such facts. Here we have existential philosophy in the
making and in its most real sense. "The book is philosophical
in conception and it is devoted to the problems of philosophy.
It is concerned with knowledge of self and with the need to
understand oneself, to discover one's own image and ultimate
destiny" (p. x). *Dream and Reality* is the book most essential
for understanding Berdyaev, the important events of his life
and the apparent contradictions in his philosophical outlook.

Truth and Revelation. Translation by R. M. French. London: Geoffrey Bles, 1953; New York: Harper & Brothers, 1954. In the opening words of the first chapter, Berdyaev assigns this book, which was published posthumously, to the realm of philosophy rather than to the field of theology. This is so even though he meant it to be "a reconsideration of the fundamental problems of Christianity in the light of spirit and truth" (p. 7). The work contains a summary of his thinking, at times revised, on some of the basic problems raised by the Christian revelation. In the light of an existential philosophical perspective, which rests on a spiritual experience, Berdyaev works out a "Critique of Revelation." He sets forth views on the relation between religion and the physical sciences, revelation and history, faith and reason. As a recipient of divine revelation, man is not passive but creatively active. Berdyaev anticipates a new birth of Christianity and warns against an optimistic belief in reason and progress as well as against a pessimistic surrender to fate and historical determinism.

The Realm of Spirit and the Realm of Caesar. Translation by Donald A. Lowrie. London: Gollancz, 1952; New York: Harper & Brothers, 1953. The manuscript of this book, Berdyaev's last, was found after his death and published posthumously. His final and most mature thoughts on a number of problems, especially collectivism, Communism, Socialism, authority, and the idea of world federation, are here presented. Berdyaev directs a devastating fire of criticism against Marxism and exposes its logical and moral contradictions. He does not hesitate to attribute the strength of Marxism "to the weakness of Christians, to the lack of expression of the realm of Spirit, which too often gives way to the realm of Caesar" (p. 150). With a prophetic intuition and courage, he proclaims that the realm of Spirit and freedom cannot be permanently subjected to that of Caesar. In his opinion, "the victory of the realm of Spirit over that of Caesar" is inevitable.

Allen, Edgar L. *Freedom in God: A Guide to the Thought of Nicolas Berdyaev*. London: Hodder & Stoughton, 1950.

—— "Nicolas Berdyaev," *Contemporary Review*, Vol. CLXXXVI (August, 1954), pp. 94–97.

Attwater, Donald (ed.). *Modern Christian Revolutionaries*. New York: The Devin-Adair Co., 1947.

Aubrey, E. E. "The Philosophy of Nicolai Berdyaev," *Theology Today*, Vol. IV (January, 1948), pp. 522–33.

Blackham, Harold John. *Six Existentialist Thinkers*. London: Routledge & Kegan Paul, 1952.

Bourke, Vernon J. "The Gnosticism of N. Berdyaev," *Thought*, Vol. XI (December, 1936), pp. 409–22.

Braybrooke, N. "Significance of Berdyaev," *Catholic World*, Vol. CLXXIV (October, 1951), pp. 409–22.

Clarke, Oliver Fielding. *Introduction to Berdyaev*. London: Geoffrey Bles, 1950.

—— "Nicolai Berdyaev 1874–1948," *Current Religious Thought* Vol. VII (April, 1948), pp. 7–10.

Fedotov, G. "Nicolas Berdyaev as Thinker," *The Living Church*, Vol. CXVII (September, 1948), pp. 15–24.

Heinemann, F. H. *Existentialism and the Modern Predicament*. London: A. & C. Black Ltd., 1953.

Kennedy, Paul. "A Philosophical Appraisal of the Modernist Gnosticism of Nicolas Berdyaev." Ph.D. Dissertation, St. Louis University, 1936.

Klamroth, Erich. *Der Gedanke der ewigen Schöpfung bei Nikolai Berdiajew*. Hamburg-Bergstedt: Herbert Reich–Evangelischer Verlag G. m. b. H., 1963.

Lampert, Evgueny. *Modern Christian Revolutionaries*, edited by Donald Attwater. London: James Clarke Ltd., 1945.

Lowrie, Donald A. *Rebellious Prophet: A Life of Nicolas Berdyaev*. London: Victor Gollancz Ltd., 1960.

Munzer, E. "Nicolas Berdyaev," *The University of Toronto Quarterly*, Vol. XIV (Spring, 1945).

Phytian-Adams, W. "Thought and Significance of Nicolas Berdyaev," *Church Quarterly Review*, Vol. CXXVI (July, 1938), pp. 245–68.

Porret, Eugene. *Nikolaj Berdjajew und die christliche Philosophie in Russland*. Heidelberg: F. H. Kerle Verlag, 1950.

Presnall, Robert E. "The Concept of Human Freedom in the Ethics of Berdyaev." Doctor's Dissertation, Southwestern Baptist Theological Seminary, Fort Worth, Texas, 1955.

Richardson, David B. "Explanation of Berdyaev's Philosophy of History." Ph.D. Dissertation, University of Toronto, 1955.

Rössler, R. *Das Weltbild Nicolai Berdjajews*. Göttingen: Vanderhoek und Ruprecht, 1956.

Rowell, E. "Meditation on Berdyaev's Three Times." *Hibbert Journal*, Vol. XLVIII (April, 1950), pp. 252–56.

Seaver, G. *Nicolas Berdyaev: An Introduction to His Thought*, London: James Clarke Ltd., 1950.

Slaatte, Howard. "Time and Its End in the Existentialism of Nicolas Berdyaev." Ph.D. Dissertation, Drew University, 1956.

Spinka, Matthew. *Nicolas Berdyaev: Captive of Freedom*. Philadelphia: The Westminster Press, 1950.

Stepun, Fedor. *Mystische Weltschau: Fünf Gestalten des russischen Symbolismus*. München: Carl Hanser Verlag, 1964.

Tillich, Paul. "Nicolas Berdyaev," *Religion in Life*, Vol. VII (Summer, 1938), pp. 407–15.

Vallon, Michel Alexander. *An Apostle of Freedom: Life and Teachings of Nicolas Berdyaev*. London: The Vision Press Ltd., 1960.

Warren, A. "A Note on Nicolas Berdyaev," *American Review*, Vol. V (1935), pp. 322–28.

Whitley, Oliver R. "Freedom, Spirit and Personality: An Introduction to the Ethics of Nicolas Berdyaev," *Encounter*, Vol. XVII, No 3 (Summer, 1956), pp. 260–71.

Williams, B. "Berdyaev's Philosophy of History." Ph.D. Dissertation, Boston University Graduate School, 1949.

Adler, Mortimer J. (ed.) *The Idea of Freedom*. New York: Doubleday & Co., 2 Volumes, 1958, 1961.

Anderson, Paul B. *People, Church and State in Modern Russia*, London: Student Christian Movement Press. Ltd., 1944.

Arseniev, Nicolas. *Mysticism and the Eastern Church*. London: 1926.

Bobbio, Norberto. *The Philosophy of Decadentism: A Study in Existentialism*. Translation by David Moore. Oxford: Basil Blackwell & Mott, Ltd., 1948.

Boehme, Jacob. *Six Theosophic Points and Other Writings*. Translation by John Rolleston Earle. New York: Alfred Knopf, 1920.

Brinton, Howard Haines. *The Mystic Will* (based on a study of the philosophy of Jacob Boehme). London: G. Allen & Co., 1931.

Bulgakov, Sergius. *The Orthodox Church*. New York: The Centenary Press, 1935.

Collins, James Daniel. *The Existentialists*. Chicago: Henry Regnery, 1952.

Frank, S. L. (arranged by), *A Solovyev Anthology*. Translation by Natalie Duddington. London: S.C.M. Press Ltd., 1950.

Grene, Marjorie. *Dreadful Freedom*. Chicago: Chicago University Press, 1948.

Grunsky, Hans Alfred. *Jacob Boehme*. Stuttgart: Fr. Frommanns Verlag, 1956.

Hegel, George Wilhelm F. *The Philosophy of History*. Translation by J. Sibree. London: W. H. Allen & Co., 1947.

Heidegger, Martin. *Sein und Zeit*. Halle: Max Niemeyer, 1927.

Heinecken, Martin J. *The Moment before God* (An Interpretation of Kierkegaard). Philadelphia: Muhlenberg Press, 1956.

Hodges, H. A. *The Philosophy of Wilhelm Dilthey.* London: Routledge & Kegan Paul Ltd., 1952.

Iswolsky, Helene. *Soul of Russia.* London: Sheed & Ward. Ltd., 1944.

Jaspers, Karl. *Man in the Modern Age.* Translation by E. and C. Paul. London: Routledge & Kegan Paul Ltd., 1933.

Kant, Immanuel. *Introduction to the Metaphysics of Morals.* Translation by Thomas Kingsmill Abbot.London: Longmans, Green & Co., 1948.

———— *The Science of Right.* Translation by W. Hastie. Great Books of the Western World, Vol. 42. Chicago: Encyclopaedia Britannica, 1952.

Kaufmann, Walter. *Existentialism: From Dostoyevsky to Sartre.* New York: Meridian Books, Inc., 1956.

Kierkegaard, Sören. *Concluding Unscientific Postscript.* Translation by David F. Swenson, completed and edited by Walter Lowrie. London: Oxford University Press, 1942.

———— *The Sickness Unto Death.* Translation by Walter Lowrie. London: Oxford University Press, 1942.

Knittermeyer, Heinrich. *Die Philosophie der Existenz.* Wien: Humboldt Verlag, 1952.

Kroner, Richard. "Existentialism and Christianity," *Encounter,* Vol. 17, No. 3. (Summer, 1956), pp. 219–44.

———— "Existential Philosophy: A Paradox," *Union Review,* Vol. VI, No. 1 (December, 1943).

———— *Kant's Weltanschauung.* Translation by John E. Smith. Chicago: University of Chicago Press, 1956.

———— *Speculation and Revelation in the Age of Christian Philosophy.* Philadelphia: The Westminster Press, 1959.

———— *Speculation and Revelation in Modern Philosophy.* Philadelphia: The Westminster Press, 1961.

———— *Von Kant bis Hegel.* Tubingen: J.C.B. Mohr (Paul Siebeck). First edition: Vol. I, 1921; Vol. II, 1923. Second editio in one volume, 1961.

Lavrin, E. B. *Russian Characteristics.* London: Chapman & Hall, 1892.

Lossky, N. O. *History of Russian Philosophy.* New York: International Universities Press, Inc., 1951.

Lowrie, Walter. *Kierkegaard*. Princeton: Princeton University Press, 1938.

Malinowski, Bronislaw. *Feedom and Civilization*. London: George Allen & Unwin Ltd., 1947.

Mannheim, Karl. *Feedom, Power and Democratic Planning*. London: Routledge & Kegan Paul, 1951.

Marcel, Gabriel. *The Mystery of Being*. 2 Volumes. London: Harvill Press Ltd., 1950–51.

—— *Being and Having*. Translation by Katherine Farrer, London: A. & C Black Ltd., 1949.

—— *The Philosophy of Existence*. Translation by Manya Harari. London: Harvill Press Ltd., 1948.

Masaryk, Thomas Garrigue. *The Spirit of Russia: Studies in History, Literature and Philosophy*. Translated from the German original by Eden and Cedar Paul. New York: The Macmillan Co., 1919.

Michalson, Carl (ed.). *Christianity and the Existentialists*. New York: Scribner's, 1956.

Moorehead, Alan. *The Russian Revolution*. London: Hamish Hamilton Ltd., 1958.

Mounier, Emmanuel. *Existentialist Philosophies*. London: Rockcliff, 1948.

Neumann, Alfred. *Dostojewski und die Freiheit*. Amsterdam: Verlag Albert De Lange, 1949.

Otto, Rudolf. *The Idea of the Holy*. Translation by John Harvey. London: Oxford University Press, 1946.

Paul, Leslie. *The Meaning of Human Existence*. London: Faber & Faber Ltd., 1949.

Read, Herbert. *Existentialism, Maxrism and Anarchism*. London: Freedom Press, 1949.

Reinhardt, Kurt Frank. *The Existentialist Revolt*. Milwaukee: Bruce Publishing Co., 1952.

Roberts, David E. *Existentialism and Reigious Belief*. London: Oxford University Press, 1960.

Ruggiero, Guido De. *Existentialism*. New York: Social Sciences Publishers, 1948.

Sartre, Jean-Paul. *Existentialism*. Translation by Bernard Frechtman. London: Methuen & Co. Ltd., 1958.

———— *Being & Nothingness*. Translation by Hazell E. Barnes. London: Methuen & Co. Ltd., 1957.

———— *The Age of Reason*. Translation by Eric Sutton. London: Hamish Hamilton Ltd., 1946.

Spoerri, Theophil. *Die Herausforderung des Existentialismus*. Hamburg: Furche-Verlag, 1954.

Thomte, Reider. *Kierkegaard's Philosophy of Religion*. Princeton: Princeton University Press, 1948.

Timasheff, N. S. *Religion in Soviet Russia*, 1917–1942, London: Sheed & Ward Ltd., 1942.

Tompkins, Stewart. *The Russian Mind*. University of Oklahoma Press, 1953.

Toynbee, Arnold. *Civilization on Trial*. London: Oxford University Press, 1948.

Ussher, Arland. *Journey Through Dread*. London: Darwen Findlayson Ltd., 1955.

Wahl, Jean. *A Short History of Existentialism*. Translated by Forrest Williams and Stanley Maron. New York: Philosophical Library, 1949.

Wild, John. *The Challenge of Existentialism*. Bloomington:Indiana University Press, 1955.

Windelband, Wilhelm. *A History of Philosophy*. Translation by James H. Tufts. New York: The Macmillan Co., 1901.

Zenkovsky, V. V. *Russian Thinkers and Europe*. Translation by G. S. Bodde. Ann Arbor, Michigan: J. W. Edward Publisher.

———— *A History of Russian Philosophy*. Translation by George L. Kline. New York: Columbia University Press, 2 Volumes, 1953.

Zernov, Nicolas. *The Church of the Eastern Christians*. London: The Society for the Propagation of Christian Knowledge, 1942.

———— *Moscow the Third Rome*. London: Society for Promoting Christian Knowledge, 1941.

———— *The Russians and Their Church*. London: Society for Promoting Christian Knowledge, 1945.

———— *Three Russian Prophets*. London: The Student Christian Movement Press Ltd., 1944.

———— *The Russian Religious Renaissance of the Twentieth Century*. London: Darton, Longman & Todd Ltd., 1963.

Zouboff, Peter P. *Godmanhood as the Main Idea of the Philosophy of Vladimir Solovyev.* Published Ph.D. Dissertation, Columbia University, 1942. New York: Harmon Printing House, 1944.